CONTROL, THE ILLUSION AND THE LIE.

The illusion is that you can have control and the lie is that you need it.

Gary Smith

CONTENTS

INTRODUCTION

This book is a journey I am on, a journey many others have joined me on, and one I will happily take you on through the following pages.

The journey is firstly about becoming conscious of how we tend to live believing that we need to be able to make life happen for us and ours. Although this may seem a responsible way to live, it actually exposes us to all sorts of unbearable pressures as we attempt to gain control over the circumstances of our everyday lives.

Once we become conscious of this, the journey then walks us out of the captivity and oppression of having to make life happen. We will be able to make peace with the circumstances of our lives and as a result discover how to engage with life in a life-giving way, for ourselves and those around us. A life that lives well in all circumstances.

the 'make it happen barrier' and the 'need to know disease'

I uncover two major problems, hidden in our human condition, that prevent us from living well. They are, 'the make it happen barrier' and 'the need-to-know disease', and they are both overcome by the journey we will go on. These are just my way of keeping it real and keeping it simple. The overall conclusion is that we can live with the hidden illusion that we can have control ourselves over the circumstances of everyday life, and the compulsive lie, that we need to have that control.

There does need to be control and order, but the fact that we feel we have to provide it is the issue. This need shows itself as fight or flight. The fighters think they can make life happen and those who flee know they can't, but fear the consequences. The behaviour of both destroys the very life it seeks to protect through control.

living freely and lightly

After twenty-five years working in industry and commerce, and twenty-seven years as a pastor; teaching, studying, praying, and experiencing 'God's kind of life', I have increasingly sought the ability to live freely and lightly in all the circumstances of everyday life. I know this is possible because Matthew quotes Jesus as saying that this is God's plan for us.

Matthew 11:28-30 The Message.

> *Come to me. Get away with me and you'll recover your life. I'll show you how to take a real rest. Walk with me and work with me—watch how I do it. Learn the unforced rhythms of grace. I won't lay anything heavy or ill-fitting on you. Keep company with me and you'll learn to live freely and lightly."*

My experience of this is that Jesus is saying that I will live freely and lightly as he does, as I become more like him. That I might less, try harder to think, speak and act as Jesus would, and more, just become like him, living freely and lightly as he says in Matthew 11 MSG. A life in all its fullness in all circumstances, good or ill, more in this world and less of it. After all these years of living, I recently said to my son, that what I want, is to be able to engage with my life in the world as Jesus would if he were I.

I found the 'way' to this kind of living in more recent years, and more simply revealed, in the beatitudes. Here, Jesus offered this pattern, or way, of becoming more like him, to a crowd of ordinary everyday people on the side of a mountain, none of whom by then could have been Christian, so that lets everyone in. He did it in a simple enough way that they would be able to live it. It took him barely ten minutes to do it, so I do wonder how it became so complicated for us.

heaven's door.

The beatitudes open heaven's door to our households, our families, our friendships and fellowships, our employment, our community, and society.

the way of open, empty, and detached

The first three beatitudes can be seen as the 'way' into transformed living (freely and lightly) that Jesus gives us to follow; to become more like him by becoming open, empty, and detached. (I will explain this fully). The remaining beatitudes, then, are some of the effects on our lives ... merciful, an undivided heart, peace-making, and righteousness. Like Jesus.

from complexity to simplicity

If living freely and lightly, by engaging with the world as Jesus would if he were I, is more simple than we have made it out to be, you may ask why do I need a book to take me there? My answer is that you don't if you can get there by living the beatitudes as they are written, like the people on the side of that mountain. The reason why you might need this book is because we live very complex lives, so this transformation is a journey we must undertake from complexity to simplicity. I will walk you there over the following pages, never straying from the simplicity of the journey.

My main belief is that the cause of Christ is that we are to be transformed to become more like him; sharing his intimate life with God the Father, and as a result, living in this world freely and lightly in all circumstances.

I'm not going to leave you at the end of this book with something to do and someplace to get to. I'm going to take you there as we journey through the book. This means that I will repeat things often throughout the book by means of review and reminders. I'm hoping you won't find this tedious. This comes about because I originated this material as a real-life journey week by week over a period of a year. Each time I gave the next message I needed to review and refer to the previous ones. In reality, most of us will forget a message we hear once, even if we're engaged and encountered at the time.

The message I'm bringing is simple and it took Jesus less than ten minutes to bring it. However, the way we live is complex so my aim is to walk us from complexity to simplicity which will take the whole of the book to achieve.

1. NATURAL TRANSFORMATION

Britain's favourite gardener said, "Plants want to grow; you just have to overcome the barriers". I think he means overcoming the barriers of drought, competition, and no food or light. I guess even Britain's favourite gardener would say you can't actually make a plant grow. Perhaps he's saying you can only do what you can, realising all the time that you are powerless to make it grow.

It's a handing over to the creator and to the circumstances of nature whilst at the same time playing our part fully. Once the barriers to growth are overcome, the plant is designed to automatically grow. I would say it's the same with people. Humans want to grow; the barriers just need to be overcome.

the kind of person we are becoming

We have in us the seeds of eternity, even divinity, I believe. By grow, I don't mean physical growth, although these things are true for physical growth too. I mean, to grow in terms of the kind of person we are becoming. To grow spiritually if you like. Growing into the kind of person that lives well in all circumstances. Once the barriers to this kind of growing are overcome, we will automatically be gradually transformed into the kind of person that lives well in all circumstances.

As with plants, once we have done everything we can do, it's a handing over to the creator and the circumstances we find ourselves in.

The fact that a barrier to growth can just be overcome and then we automatically grow, may go against the idea that we must have an answer, or even a religious answer, for every issue in our daily lives and apply that answer in order to grow. This would require an impossible amount of religious knowledge and certainly exclude me. But when Jesus spoke to a crowd of ordinary everyday people on the side of a mountain, in the sermon on the mount, he shared three short pathways of 'the way' to overcome the barriers to living well, and he believed it to be enough for them to practice that and begin to find a whole new kind of life.

*it's just one answer for all the
circumstances of everyday life.*

That one answer is to become like him. Or as Paul says in Philippians 2, "*you must have the same mind as Christ*". I'll develop this later.

the 'make it happen' barrier

I'm calling the barrier that needs to be overcome, in order to grow into the kind of person that lives well in all circumstances, the 'make it happen' barrier. I believe this is what Jesus is talking about in the first beatitude. It's very simple to understand but proves to be the hardest thing we'll ever do. We find ourselves in a life that is very complex so this is a journey from complexity to simplicity. Not so much simplifying the way we live, which I understand is a good thing, but simplifying who we are becoming and therefore simplifying how we engage with everyday life. As I said earlier this only requires one thing, the journey of becoming more like him.

are we up for it?

We'll need God's power, which is why in the first beatitude Jesus promises 'theirs is the kingdom of heaven'. Jesus felt it was achievable and shows us how in his central message of the beatitudes from the sermon on the mount; three short pathways of the 'way' into a transformed life. I'm not talking about the idea of three steps for this or five steps for that. That sounds like a self-help remedy, which I wouldn't disagree with, but this isn't that.

I'm identifying one barrier to growth. The 'make it happen barrier' which grows from the seed of us wanting to gain control over our lives. I'm not proposing a therapy approach that would be the role of a professional therapist which I'm not. A therapy approach may require analysing specific problems like say behaviour, habits or difficult circumstances. In therapy, all these problems and more may require each one to be carefully identified and a specific remedy being found and applied for each. Even now I feel like I'm standing on the toes of professionals so I'll leave the therapy in their capable hands.

anxiety issues

An example of this for me would be when I'm not living well in the circumstances of my everyday life because I have anxiety issues. Therefore, I may feel I need to examine where those issues are coming from, usually the fear of things going out of my control, and then engage in a therapeutic route to fix the anxiety problems. I have done this and it is responsible to do it, but as my therapist said, therapy can identify the possible causes and some good behaviour patterns to relieve the symptoms but I can't heal you of the cause, the infirmity. The result is that I'm engaging with the circumstances of my everyday life poorly as a result of my life experience, which probably all of us do, as a result of the kind of person I am becoming.

> *'I can deal with your symptoms but I can't heal who you have become'*

This is where the change comes. As my anxiety therapist said 'I can deal with your symptoms but I can't heal who you have become'. She identified how the long-term circumstances of my everyday life had formed me, from a very young age, to need to be self-sufficient, to be able to make life happen because I believed no one else would.

I found this diagnosis very helpful. It gave me a story, a reason for how I am like I am. There is something wrong with my behaviour that is damaging my experience of living, yes, but my behaviour is merely a symptom of the way I tick, the kind of person I am becoming. My behaviour is just being directed by who I am, my soul if you like. As my behaviour is a symptom of who I am becoming there is no point in just trying to behave better. Have you noticed; it just doesn't work? I need a healing of my soul.

no fault or blame

This is why Jesus doesn't address our behaviour, and doesn't tell us to clean up our act. He knows we can't. There is something wrong with the formation of who I am and it's common to all humanity. We are all formed by our life experience to date. Jesus doesn't look for fault or blame. There are not two queues of people, one for whose fault it was and another for those who suffer through the fault of others. Equally, although we like to make lists of all the types of people there are, to make sure we're being inclusive, to Jesus we're all the same. We were never un-included.

"Come to me all you who are weary" Matt 11:28 NIV.

So instead of addressing how we all got to this place in our lives, Jesus instead is addressing who we are all becoming from now on, by making it possible for us to become more like him. Then our behaviour and the way we live our lives will automatically change as I indicated earlier in the chapter.

one thing to address all things.

What if there was one thing, I could address, that would

transform the way I tick and transform the kind of person I am becoming; one thing to address everything else and allow me to live freely and lightly in all circumstances, as Jesus says in Mathew 11:28-30 MSG. The one thing that is debilitating my experience of living is the hidden underlying belief that I have to make life happen. The 'make it happen barrier'. The belief that remedies are needed for all the issues of everyday life. This is the underlying cause of my poor experience of living, manifested in anxiety and poor behaviour.

Having the need to make life happen could just as easily be manifested as anger, fear, withdrawal, zeal, pushiness, self-promoting, obsessively needing to resolve problems or, compulsive pleasure-seeking. I need to make myself happy, or I need to make my family happy. I need to solve all their problems and I need to make things work out how I feel I need them to work out for me and mine.

Apparently, it's normal for us to believe that we're on our own in the world and that if we don't establish control over our lives then things will go out of control. I think it's instinctive and that we're all born with it as a survival mechanism, but left to itself, it is the barrier to our growth into the kind of person that lives well in all circumstances.

overcoming the 'make it happen barrier'.

'make it happen' people are seen as successful

'Make it happen' people are seen as successful in our society but in reality, it's an illusion, we can't make life happen.

> *The 'make it happen' barrier is less a problem to be fixed and more something that can be overtaken by something else.*

This alters the way it is addressed. Fixing requires a multitude of remedies whereas overtaking requires investing in something else. In the first of the first three beatitudes in Matthew 5, Jesus offers the 'something else' the way to overtake the 'make it happen barrier' and begin our transformation into the kind of person who lives well in all circumstances. Jesus is talking to a crowd of ordinary everyday people on the side of a mountain. He's saying, this is the 'way' to live life in all its fullness, walk in it.

Now, either Jesus is only talking to a small part of humanity, or we all have this condition. My experience tells me that we either; believe we can make life happen when it's needed, in which case we blindly go for it, or, we believe we can't make life happen when it's needed and things will just spin out of control, so we give up defeated. Either way, our behaviour is driven by the need to make life happen when the issues of everyday life arise.

blessed are the poor in spirit

The first of the three beatitudes that overtake the 'make it happen barrier' by transforming us, is where Jesus in Matthew 5:3 says,

> "Blessed are the poor in spirit for theirs is the Kingdom of Heaven"

Translated this can be... blessed are those who realise they are powerless to make life happen, the poor in spirit, for they will inherit the power of God (Kingdom of Heaven) in their everyday lives.

Remember this is Jesus calling us to become like him who in Philippians 2:5-7, set aside the power to make life happen, which he possessed, to become like us, powerless, the poor in spirit, so that we can become like him, reliant on the Father. Yes, Jesus is describing himself as the poor in spirit. Is that a new thought for you?

Realising his powerlessness however for Jesus was not an excuse to sit back and do nothing, he was very active.

Can you remember I said earlier that Jesus knows we will need the power of God for this transformation, well here it is? "Theirs is the Kingdom of heaven". So, when Jesus was faced with the circumstances of everyday life, he did everything he could while realising his powerlessness to make life happen.

the journey from complexity to simplicity begins here.

The journey of transforming us into the kind of person who lives well in all circumstances, like Jesus. To become more like him as the circumstances of everyday life come, we are to do everything we can while realising our powerlessness to make life happen. This will probably be a whole new idea for you. But it's plainly there in the first beatitude. How did we miss it? Perhaps you didn't. I did.

I'm going to leave you with an exercise, for now, that will help you on your journey of transformation, to overcome the 'make it happen barrier'

The exercise

overcoming the 'make it happen' barrier.

As the issues of everyday life arise, I must do everything I can while all the time realising, I'm powerless to make life happen.

Practicing this will enable you to avoid taking on the burden of trying to make life happen. Remember this is the first beatitude. Practice this exercise repeatedly every day, every time the issues of life come which they surely will. I'm offering you one thing to do simply, just like Jesus offered it to those ordinary everyday people on the side of a mountain. No more books to read, no studies, no analysis, just trust the beatitude to begin its work. Jesus did.

The biblical basis for this exercise is that when Jesus came, he surrendered his power and instead, in all circumstances, did everything he could, realising all the time his own powerlessness to make life happen. This opened the way for his Father's power in his life, the kingdom of heaven, which he chose to depend totally upon, as we will if we follow him in this.

called to become like him

So, in this way, we are less called to do what Jesus would do in every circumstance, which would be impossible to remember, and more, called to become like him. As Paul says "you must have the mind of Christ". We will then automatically think, speak and act as he would if he were us. I will develop this more later.

This exercise is the first of three pathways to becoming like him. Becoming more like him, we will automatically think what he would think, say what he would say, and do what he would do. I'm speaking less of a mission or ministry perspective here, and more about the way we engage with everyday life which will in turn impact us and the world around us.

The 'make it happen barrier' will be overcome and we can begin to grow more and more like him, enabling us to live his kind of life, freely and lightly as Matthew says in Matthew 11:30 MSG.

Practicing this simple exercise is a choice we will make every day, several times a day, as the Father transforms us to become like Jesus who lives well in all circumstances. Three years after this discovery I'm still having to practice this first beatitude constantly as the issues of everyday life come.

it's gradually becoming automatic; it's becoming who I am, not what I do.

I, and others I have had the pleasure to lead, are finding sufficient breakthrough, in terms of living better in all circumstances, to keep going. It's becoming who we are. More like Jesus. But every day requires us to live this first beatitude all over again as Jesus did.

Most days I often find myself living poorly in some way, but now I know what to practice to change that. I can dare to say I am becoming more like him day by day and in as much as I do become more like him, I can live well whatever comes.

In the next chapter I will reveal how realising our own powerlessness to make life happen, is less a defeated giving up or giving in, to the circumstances of life, and more a wise giving way to a new kind of life and a greater power than ours, for theirs is the kingdom of heaven.

your own summary

The teachings in these chapters were given progressively over a period of time and I have also used them as a weekly or fortnightly spiritual direction journey which gives time to reflect before moving on. Can I suggest that you scan over this chapter and make a list of some of the main things you've discovered? Can I also encourage you to begin practicing the exercise which will become true as you practice it?

The reason I am giving you a simple exercise is that this is less an idea that is understood and more a path that we must walk.

The exercise will engage you in walking the beatitudes into your life. Please don't be put off by how simple the exercise is. People before you have experienced profound encounters with God through it. I still practice this exercise but it has now become more a part of who I am becoming so it comes natural to me.

The exercise again

overcoming the make it happen barrier.

As the issues of everyday life arise, I must do everything I can while all the time realising, I'm powerless to make life happen.

2. POWERLESSNESS AS THE PATHWAY TO LIVING FREELY AND LIGHTLY IN ALL CIRCUMSTANCES

This chapter raises a multitude of questions which I will address later so you will find me continuing to say, I'll show you later, quite a lot in this chapter. Please bear with me, I've been all the way through and taken others on the same journey.

We're still with the first beatitude,

"blessed are the poor in spirit for theirs
is the Kingdom of heaven".

At the time I was teaching this we had a diagnosis of serious illness in the family. I very quickly felt powerless. I was shocked by the diagnosis but the realisation of my powerlessness to make something happen came as a blessing. By realisation, I mean embracing the reality. I leaned into everything the health professionals offered, with gratitude, and at the same time, I leaned in very closely to God. I was totally handed over to both.

About a year later we were house hunting and I didn't realise my powerlessness to make that happen. I got far too involved in trying to make it happen. We went through two house purchases that fell through before we managed to buy a house and I experienced a lot of self-imposed anxiety. A self-imposed exile you might say, as all the Old Testament exiles were. I found life in a serious illness diagnosis but less so in a house move.

realising our powerlessness is embracing reality.

Realising our powerlessness to make life happen in the circumstances of everyday life is a big ask for most people and the way I will explain it, it's probably a big ask for all people. It will take a lot of practice. Remember it is the first of three pathways on the journey towards living freely and lightly as Jesus gave us in the beatitudes. Powerlessness is the pathway to experiencing God's presence and power in our everyday lives.

but surely, I do have power over the circumstances of everyday life

My guess is that we may feel we don't agree with the idea of powerlessness because we look at things and think, yeah, if I do certain things then I believe I can make things happen. At one level that can be true but at the level of making things happen in the circumstances of our lives it is not true, it's an illusion, as I will explain.

One of the reasons we may reject our powerlessness is because there are things we can do, and need to do. I will also come to that because we will need to still do everything we can whilst realising all the time our powerlessness to make life happen. Realising our powerlessness is the essence of the first beatitude and is the doorway to experiencing a new kind of life. It's a doorway to experiencing a power higher than our own called the kingdom of heaven, as promised in the first beatitude.

the illusion of our power over circumstance

For example, if I work and get paid, I can make provision for my family or establish a household for myself. I appear to have power over that. But circumstances may mean that my job comes under threat and keeping my job may not be something I can make happen. As soon as I take upon myself the idea that I must make this happen, I must be able to keep my job, I experience threat. Threat affects my behaviour. Instinctively, I will either fight or flee. Included in flee, would be to just give up defeated. My ability to make sound judgements and relate to people is run down. So, I can't make good decisions about the future and my relationships with my family and friends may well come under pressure or even breakdown. I fill up on things like guilt, shame and entitlement as they raise their ugly heads. I'll talk about entitlement later. Even as I write this, I'm picking up some measure of threat for myself or my family. It is quite compelling. As soon as I take it upon myself to make life happen, I begin the trespass away from the higher power, God, which is why it feels so desperate. Forgive us our trespasses.

Because I'm engaging with the threat of job loss on the basis that I have to make something happen, my reactions become destructive to the very things I feel I need to save; the well-being of my household. What I need to do, according to the first beatitude, is to do everything I can to maintain a livelihood while realising my powerlessness to make it happen.

respond or react

I then become responsive to my circumstances and to how God is working for me, as opposed to being reactive. I become response-able. I'll explain later. Perhaps I can leave you to identify a similar example in your own life where the circumstances you are under pressurise you to believe that you have to make something happen, or that you should, but can't. It could be in the areas of say, health, wealth, relationships, and schooling for your kids or whatever. I find it even harder when it affects someone else that I care about. Sufficient to say that in the circumstances of everyday life we are ultimately powerless to make life happen.

holding out on the idea of powerlessness.

You may still be holding out on the idea of our powerlessness and often I still find myself doing the same but I know where to go with it. I often get the sense that I really need to make something happen and I engage with the circumstances on that basis. The danger sign for me is raised anxiety and a deterioration in my behaviour, as I fear that I might not be able to pull this off. It can be something for me or for someone I feel responsible for. Compulsion and obsession appear in my behaviour. The effect can be so severe that I can feel quickly overwhelmed and dizzy. I can interfere firstly in my mind, then my words, then my actions. It's like an unstoppable force. I may feel the need to talk over people and even infer that they need to act or even think in a way I feel is needed.

I almost always project the issue into the future seeing problems and creating schemes to resolve them. I'm trespassing and I'm on the run. It looks like I'm being proactive but it's a fear of things going out of my control. Initially, it's the fight instinct pushing for certainty, and it quickly becomes the flight instinct, as I believe that if I can't make this happen then things will spin out of control. If I can't see a way through then subconsciously, I believe there is no way through. Forgive us our trespasses.

behaviour deterioration.

You can easily see why my behaviour will deteriorate as soon as I believe that in a circumstance of everyday life, I feel I need to make life happen. I become harsh, insensitive to those around me, overwhelmed, dizzy, anxious, and destructive to the very thing I'm trying to save. Jesus says this very thing here.

> "For whoever wants to save their life will lose it". Matt 16:25 NIV.

My ability to see clearly has gone when I need it most. I have no wisdom, no insight; I'm well and truly lost. I'm no use to myself or anyone else. Worse, I am becoming a liability.

Living like this creates the kind of person we are becoming. Some of us fight and some of us flee. It's the same condition. Defeat is always the outcome in the end. I've lived like this for most of my life and it's worked some unhelpful thinking and behaviour patterns into me. The most dangerous time is when making things happen works in the short term. But the cost of who I am becoming is not seen until later and of course, I never see the outcomes that could have come from a different approach.

I am the subject of my early years.

For most of the early part of my life, I was taught to be the kind of person who must be able to make life happen in all circumstances. It was encouraged and society rewarded it. The burden of responsibility however took its toll on my psychological health and in my behaviour patterns; the sort of person I was becoming. It wasn't until I became older that I realised how unnecessary and harmful it was.

This instinct is essential for survival in terms of, if I put my hand in a fire, I will withdraw it. I can make that happen. But we were made for a higher level of living than this. In the bible, Jesus calls it, life in all its fullness, and living freely and lightly. This is where we are headed.

In the process, we will be transformed into becoming more like Jesus, the kind of person that lives well in all circumstances, which is God's intention for us and quite possibly in my mind, the good news of the Gospel. The kingdom cause of Christ.

what does Jesus have to say about all this

"Blessed are the poor in spirit for theirs is the kingdom of heaven". Matthew 5:3 NIV

Eugene Peterson breaks into the mystery of this in the Message Bible. He translates this beatitude as,

"blessed are you when you're at the end of your rope".

When you've done everything you can, and realise you are powerless to make life happen, at the end of your rope, then you are blessed. It doesn't sound like a blessing, does it? However, if we have never practiced doing everything we can while realising our powerlessness to make life happen, we wouldn't know the blessing, would we? How on earth did we miss the simplicity of this. It's less, giving up or giving in and more, giving way.

heaven's door.

A realisation of powerlessness gives way to the "kingdom of heaven" according to the text. My kingdom, for God's Kingdom. My way for God's way. My ideas for God's ideas. My power for God's power. Not by trying to remember God's ways for everything but by becoming more like him and automatically knowing his ways. Realising my powerlessness to make life happen literally opens heaven's door for me, for my household, for my community, and for society.

If I subconsciously believe I have a chance to make something happen, like a house purchase, I will never realise the truth of my powerlessness to make something happen. In this state, I have become closed to the presence and power of God and have placed myself on a course of defeat. Trespassing. It's just a matter of time. A self-imposed exile from God's presence just like all those self-imposed exiles in the Old Testament.

the blessed place of openness.

In giving way to the reality of my powerlessness to make life happen, I'm no longer faced with just giving up or giving in, and I become open to God's presence and power. I've heard it called the blessed place of openness. When a vessel is closed it can't receive anything, it can only receive when it's open. Blindly obvious, but then again, refusing to realise my powerless to make life happen, closes me and blinds me.

The summary of this chapter is for us to become open to our own powerlessness to make life happen, which then opens us to God's presence and power for a new kind of living; living freely and lightly in all circumstances. For theirs is the Kingdom of Heaven.

who is this like?

He didn't cling to equality with God but chose to become like us, powerless to make life happen and fully open to his father's presence and power. Jesus.

I'm hoping by now that you're beginning to see that realising our powerlessness to make life happen is not a weak thing. When we do everything we can, as the issues of life come, realising all the time our powerlessness to make life happen, we become open to God's very presence. His thoughts. His ways. New ways through life's circumstances. (for theirs is the Kingdom of Heaven). I have found this to be so true in my employment in industry and business and then later in planting and leading a church. The final territory for me is to find a greater measure of freedom in my home life. My family are wonderful, but I still perceive threats and challenges to us in our ordinary everyday lives. I am however finding freedom here too, slowly but surely. I just tend to feel more vulnerable when it's my family. Perhaps you may choose to join me on this journey.

theirs is the Kingdom of Heaven

The theologies for the Kingdom of Heaven are well known and that's not the purpose of this book. But what is the Kingdom of Heaven like in reality, now for me, for the person in front of me? The simplest reality I think is that the Kingdom of Heaven is where we experience the flow of an eternal kind of life into every part of our lives, the brokenness, and the beauty, bathing every wound, satisfying every thirst, and bringing life in all its fullness.

It's where God works for the good in all things for those who love him and are called according to his purpose. Romans 8:28 NIV (His purpose being to transform our kind of life into his kind of life).

For a time, I communicated this incorrectly. I said that God makes good of all things, which could lead to thinking that God fixes everything. But the scripture doesn't say God makes good it actually says … God works for the good in all things. It's not the same. Have a think about it. Believing that God makes good of everything, and fixes everything, is not theologically correct and leads us on a wild goose chase of unmet expectations which will erode our faith.

powerlessness, fight it or embrace it.

So, the Kingdom of heaven is where God works for the good in all the things the world throws at us, all things that people throw at us, all things that life throws at us, and all things we throw at ourselves; he even works for the good in death. God works for the good in all things and when you get that feeling of powerlessness there is a choice to fight it or embrace it.

According to Jesus, for us to experience the flow of God's Kingdom of Heaven life, working for the good in all things, we must, having done everything we can, realising our powerlessness to make life happen. This is how we become the poor in spirit and receive the goodness of God working for the good in all things.

What does 'all things' leave out? Nothing. In our diagnosis of serious illness, I did just this, automatically, and experienced God bringing peace, avoiding life-destroying obsessive involvements, reactions, retaliations, and battles. Although it was in no way easy and it was painful.

In our house buying, I did the opposite. I guess I subconsciously rejected powerlessness and began the fight to make good of all things myself. The territory of deity. Subconsciously I thought I had a shot at making it happen. I wrongly believed I needed to have control over it.

Hidden among some good behaviour I reacted poorly, I pushed, I retaliated, and I tried to influence, and manipulate. I spent too much time, wasted too much of my daily bread life, and became depleted and almost defeated. Eventually, reaching the end of my rope, I did everything I could and embraced my powerlessness, and found a light burden and easy yoke. Matt 11:30 NIV.

the great unravelling

Doing what I could, not trying to make things happen, I was standing in the life-stream of God's life, as opposed to standing in the traffic and getting cut to pieces. Yes, needing control over making life happen is like standing in traffic and getting cut to pieces. Our lives unravel every day in the experience of everyday life, but as we embrace our powerlessness to make life happen, we see that God is weaving it all back together working for the good in all things.

The Greek word for this is kartismos, the word the gospel writers borrowed from the mending of fishing nets. We may not realise that our life up to date has formed us in a fractured way, to react poorly to the circumstances of life. Like a fractured well that leaks water. Jeremiah 2:13, Paul Romans 7:19 or a fractured net that lets the very life it seeks to catch, escape from it. This is often without our realisation or consent; we can't help it. It wreaks havoc in our lives and in the lives of those around us. From our fractured life experience, even our God-given desires are headed off the course of blessing us and others, and into a destructive and possibly depraved path. Have a think about that.

As we live open to our powerlessness to make life happen, in the Kingdom of Heaven's life-stream, however, the things that fracture us are overtaken by a new life in formation that brings life into the whole of our experience of living, into our troubles and our pleasures. The kingdom life flow shows itself in how we feel, think, speak and act as I indicated in my own experiences.

so, the only question now is ... will we choose
to become the poor in spirit?

The poor in spirit are those who choose to embrace their powerlessness to make life happen and inherit the kingdom of heaven; the flow of God's life overtaking fractured lives, re-creating us into the kind of people who live well in all circumstances.

Note, that Jesus chose powerlessness even though he had the power to make anything happen. In the same way we are called to choose powerlessness to make life happen while all the time still doing everything we can. We fulfill our responsibilities by doing everything we can but in the freedom of realising our powerlessness to make things happen. This frees us from the captivity of being connected to the need to create the specific outcomes of our own devices. This freedom is then found in all areas of life like work, play, household, community, and society as I will show you later. Perhaps like me, in some areas, we readily surrender and in others not.

it's time for another exercise.

This exercise adds to the first exercise the line, "God is working for the good in all things". Here it is.

In the circumstances of everyday life, God is working for the
good in all things, as I do everything I can while realising my
powerlessness to make life happen.

Practice this every day, several times a day, in and amongst the circumstances of your everyday life. It will soon become a part of you. God will begin to renew your feelings, thoughts, words, and your actions, and the world around you through you.

Again, as before, why not make a short list of what you thought were the major points in this chapter. These teachings were given with space in between to practice the exercises so you may need to reflect for a few days or a week before moving to chapter 3.

3. THE THINGS THAT CONTROL US AND BREAKING FREE FROM THEM.

I n this chapter, we're heading into the second beatitude, and after this, there is only one more to go. You will in no way have mastered the first beatitude by now but if you've practiced it, you will be ready for the second. Remember the first beatitude is the blessed place of openness, open to God.

The first three beatitudes are constantly repeated pathways in a walk. A 'way' of walking if you like, through everyday life. One step follows the other and makes way for the next. So, you can't just jump to the second beatitude ignoring the first. If the first beatitude is the blessed state of openness, then the second is the blessed state of emptiness.

A container, in order to be filled, has to be open and empty. A nice simple thing to understand. The second beatitude then is ….

> *"Blessed are those who mourn, for they will be comforted". Matthew 5:4 NIV*

In this chapter I will introduce self-emptying from the text.

Mourn = Kenos = Empty.

The word used in the text as mourn is derived from the word kenos. Kenos means empty. So, the beatitude would then be;

blessed are those who are empty for they will be comforted.

Kenosis is the word used when Jesus emptied himself of his entitlement to equality with God as Paul says in Philippians 2. And the walk Jesus took in his life, whereby he experienced his father's presence and power, that we're called to join him on, is called the kenotic path. Can you now see that the 'way' we are to follow Jesus, is by becoming like him? The word Jesus used for us to walk this way, kenos/mourn, is the same word used of Jesus' self-emptying, of his entitlement to equality with God. This theme is also picked up when Jesus says in Matthew 11:29 MSG

> *"walk with me work with me – watch how I do it. Learn the unforced rhythms of grace. I won't lay anything heavy or ill-fitting on you".*

This is the self-emptying, kenotic path. That's how Jesus did it, that's how we are called to do it. So, why do we need to self-empty, how do we do it and what do we self-empty ourselves of?

control, the illusion and the lie

Remember Jesus needed to self-empty himself of equality with God to become like us so that we might become like him and live freely and lightly. The reason we need to self-empty is because we are living with the effects of the illusion that we can have control over our own lives and the lie that we need to. This is our unintended belief that we have equality with God and can control our own lives. We have not generally realised our powerlessness to make life happen. The reasons may be good or poor. It's not basically bad to be compelled to establish control over the circumstances that you or your family are experiencing. But as detailed in the first beatitude this traps us in our own devices and closes us to how God will be working for us. We're in effect going it alone.

the modern phrase for this is 'I've got this'.

Living under the illusion that we can and must have control over our own lives fills us up with all sorts of expectations or needs. We expect things to get sorted. It also fills us up with the entitlement to better things. When circumstances don't go the way we feel we really need or deserve them to go, we can fill up with disappointment, disillusionment, resentfulness, bitterness, anger, or just plain hurt. These are what we need to self-empty. The things that we have inadvertently filled ourselves up with, control us. We have given them power over us. The bible talks about the tyranny of powers, well these are they. Eph 6:12. They in effect poison us. They control our behaviour, our mood, our psychological condition, and our physical and mental health. This is why we need to self-empty ourselves of them.

The reason we know that they control us is because in the second beatitude Jesus says that those who mourn/self-empty will be comforted. Held by God instead of being held by our stuff.

> *"Blessed are those who mourn for they shall be comforted".*
> *Matthew 5:4 NIV*

the practice of self-emptying

The practice of self-emptying, mourning, is more than a release from troubles, it's a release from all the things that control us. A walk of self-emptying is where we learn to empty ourselves of our hopes and dreams as well as our troubles and losses. We can and must have hopes and dreams, but when we use them to try to control the future, they become poison and we've given them power to control us.

Remember just like embracing the moment of powerlessness is a blessing, so is engaging in the process of self-emptying/ mourning. Again, it's the opposite of what our lives so far might have taught us.

So, we now know what we need to self-empty ourselves of, and why. You might want to read back a little way to make sure you can see this. The question now is how?

self-emptying requires the embrace of powerlessness.

Take note that in the beatitudes, self-emptying/mourning, comes after the first beatitude,

doing everything we can while realising our powerlessness to make life happen.

This breaks the illusion that we can have control over our own lives and that we need it. Only as we realise our powerlessness to make life happen and find that place of freedom, will we be ready, and have the power of the kingdom of heaven, to self-empty. Whilst ever we avoid powerlessness, we avoid the place of freedom from our need for control and we fill up with things in our lives that then have power over us and control us.

but these things we are to self-empty
are important, aren't they?

At this point, the question arises that surely, it's only right to stick out for the things I need or my family needs. Well of course it is important and God knows it's important. But we'll never know how to engage with the issues of life in a life-giving way while we live under the illusion that we can have control over them and believe the lie that we need to have control over them. That's so important I'll make a quote of it here.

we'll never know how to engage with the issues of life in a life-giving way while we live under the illusion that we can have control over them and believe the lie that we need to have control over them.

This is why we must walk the beatitudes path to become more like

Jesus, the poor in spirit. *We must always do everything can but at the same time realise we're powerless to make life happen.*

With the noise in our heads quietened in this place of openness it will become clear what we have allowed in that needs to be self-emptied. Practicing the first beatitude in this way will empower us to practice the second, and self-empty. It's only then that we even know what to self-empty. Once it's revealed to us what is poisoning us, we will automatically empty ourselves of it. We will literally throw it out as the abhorrence it is. The entitlement to something better, the disappointment, disillusionment, resentfulness, bitterness, anger, or just plain hurt. Whatever it is we will know it must go.

I wouldn't go fishing from the list and try to self-empty any of these things. It will be revealed to us what needs to come out as we practice powerlessness and if it isn't at first then wait until it is. I believe this is an authentic encounter with God and not a therapeutic response. There's nothing wrong with a therapeutic response but this is not that. Remember I'm not a therapist. When it comes it's a wonderful release from the power of being controlled by these things.

self-emptying is not letting go.

Self-emptying makes way for us to let go of something else that is holding us but that's the subject of the third and final beatitude of the three, life-transforming beatitudes.

Sometimes I walk the beatitudes, sometimes I don't.
When the moment of powerlessness came with our serious illness diagnosis, we automatically embraced our powerlessness. That opened the door to the eternal kind of life of God flowing into our experience. It was a mysterious time. With heaven's door open we were then released into a walk of self-emptying of hopes and fears. We avoided the need to have control over our days, and so were not ruled by our fears, hopes, and dreams. It was still a shock and it

still hurt but it didn't take us prisoner.

fractured living

With house moving however I didn't perceive the moments of powerlessness at first. In my mind, I was just playing my part and doing the things you need to do but in reality, I was full of ways I could help things along, to make things happen. I fell for the illusion that I could have full control over the house purchase and believed the lie that I needed to have that control. All because I missed the moments of powerlessness. Without realising those moments of powerlessness, I had no discernment of what to do and what to leave out. So, I tended to overdo, resenting those who didn't do what I thought they should do.

Note, I filled up with the poison of resentment which made me vulnerable. And leaving heaven's door closed on my side I was completely blind to self-emptying my vulnerabilities. In fact, I was totally unaware of them. Quite the opposite I was filling up with what I could do to make things happen and bring about this illusion of control.

There was no flow here of God's eternal kind of life, no 'theirs is the Kingdom of heaven', and no life-giving embrace of the father. I was living my kind of life instead of living Jesus' kind of life. I was living out of who I had become, instead of living out of who I would be becoming by following the Jesus way, the beatitudes.

Without embracing the moment of powerlessness, I left heaven's door closed so I was burning my own limited strength instead of the inexhaustible energy of God. The effect of me burning my own life energy instead of God's grace, was debilitation, loss of peace, suspicion, fear, and threat of loss. This was no preparation for when we lost two houses we had surveyed and I had spent so much of myself on. There was a price to pay apart from the unnecessary bills, of lowered immunity and sickness, compulsiveness, obsession, and anxiety.

These are the effects of the self-administered poisons I spoke of earlier. Entitlement, resentment, hurt, fear, fantasy, just about anything that might come as I sought to bring about the illusion of control. All these worked their way into my mood resulting in my behaviour deteriorating. All in all, a really poor experience of living. I was holding onto the need to make it happen and it was holding me. A perfect example of a very poor way of living.

mending the nets, kartismos

Thankfully Jesus is constantly knocking on heaven's door from his side and eventually, I heard him and opened the door by embracing the reality of the moments of powerlessness that inevitably came. Everything changed. I was able to discern what was mine to do and do only that. I was awakened to engage in the process of self-emptying/mourning. I emptied out the need, the entitlement, for this thing to happen. Sensitivity to others returned, peace was coming, suspicion was going, and fears and the threat of loss were fading. My general health recovered.

 I have used these examples from my own life to reveal how the life of God can flow and how it can so easily be prevented. Now it's over to you to consider this question.

> In the circumstances of everyday life, can you practice the first beatitude and do everything you can while realising your powerlessness to make life happen?

and

> As you discern those moments of powerlessness will you embrace them and with the flow of life that will come, engage in a walk of self-emptying, mourning.

more about self-emptying/mourning

Remember, not realising our own powerlessness closes us to what could be. Psychologists and spiritual teachers often agree on this. It's like a stopper in a bottle in which these vested interests are now brewing up inside, with the inevitable result. The bottle experiences significant pressure and eventually breaks.

You can see this displayed in sports like tennis where there is an illusion that you can have control over winning, you just have to make this happen.

the telling phrase is "I've got this".

On losing, or even before losing, the bottle bursts under the pressure. A sports person that wants to win and does everything they possibly can to win but realises their powerlessness to actually make that happen, will survive and grow and find pleasure in their sport. They may well even win more often. I've seen world-class tennis players defeat themselves in effect even before the game begins by their absolute belief that they have to make winning happen. The pressure blinds them to their well-practiced skills and the psyche hammers the body such that it cannot perform at the levels of freedom they enjoy in practice.

Control, the illusion and the lie. The illusion is that you can have control and the lie is that you need it.

It's the same for all of us in everyday life. We will often carry the 'make it happen' burden to get the job, find the partner, win, or just have to make something happen for us or for our loved ones, to get through the situation we are facing. In as much as we attempt these everyday life things without the beatitudes, like the sportspeople, our psyche will hammer our body so that we just cannot perform. Been there, done that, still do it sometimes. The problem with living with the illusion that we can have control over making life happen is that we are destined to be dis – illusioned. We are blinded to the wisdom that would come to us, and our physical and mental health carries the scars of the pressure in the bottle. Fractures, cracks, and sometimes an outburst, explosion, or even a breakdown.

the danger of entitlement

So, I'm still talking about when we do not realise our powerlessness to make life happen, we become like a closed bottle and we fill up on vulnerabilities, like the dreaded curse of entitlement, and other sensitivities. I have used this material in spiritual direction both as a full course and by dipping into main truths like this one.

On one occasion I was sharing some of this with a head of research in a large company who was receiving the high level of psychotherapy these big companies provide. The therapist became aware of the things I was sharing and said "this is good can I use it". My thought was, as long as you credit the author …. Jesus in the beatitudes.

The danger of entitlement is that it's perfectly understandable to think that we're entitled to better than we're receiving. I deserve to be treated better than this. I deserve better rewards. I deserve to be respected or obeyed. I deserve to be well. We may well be entitled to these things, but allowing that entitlement into us, will poison us. Have a think about how you may have experienced this. I believe you must have if you've been on the planet for more than ten minutes. Have a think about how holding onto your entitlements or your need to be in control of how things work out, worked out.

entitlement in action, the wedding address.

On the occasions I've given a wedding address, I also address the parents of the bride and groom. It goes like this. When your kids were young, they were called to obey their parents. However, when embarking on a life with a partner for life, your kids are called instead to honour their parents. Eph 6:1-3. So, in order for the kids to be able to honour their parents, the parents must give up their entitlement to tell their kids what to do. There are usually a few knowing smiles at this point. It always goes down well though and I get really good feedback for this.

from my life in industry and commerce.

When working in industry and commerce I sometimes found myself being treated less well than perhaps I should have been. The journey through my working life overall has been very fruitful. However, there were times when I was taken advantage of, falsely accused, overlooked, and under-rewarded. I guess this happens in all areas of daily living; at home, in the community, and even possibly in the church. Although I have always found my experience of the local church to be a growing experience of affirmation, affection, and freedom.

powerless to defend

In my time in industry and commerce of some twenty-five years, I inadvertently discovered the practice of *doing everything I could while realising my powerlessness to make life happen.* So, when wrongly accused of things, and when appropriate, I offered my defence, which was either accepted or rejected. Often my defence was rejected but I settled, in my powerlessness to make my defence happen. I found myself to be in a place of peace as opposed to bearing a grudge, which would literally eat you.

powerless to win rewards

Another example was being under-rewarded on salary. This happened on three occasions and doing everything I could included petitioning my boss graciously. On one of those occasions, the business I managed had done very well indeed and I anticipated an appropriate pay rise at the end of the year. That year I received the lowest percentage pay rise I'd ever had and lower than the rises I was able to award to my staff for their performance. I asked my boss how he thought the pay rise reflected the increase in profit I delivered. This was me doing everything I could do and then realising my powerlessness to make it happen. I also said that at the end of the day it was the company's responsibility to make the pay rises they felt appropriate and I'd leave that with him. I emptied myself of the entitlement. I bore no grudge, surprising myself with that. There was nothing in me to ferment into a grievance, I was free.

a reward and a wound

The first beatitude of realising my powerlessness had worked for me and made way for the second, self-emptying my entitlement which also worked. I guess you want to know what happened next. Well, my boss then immediately left and I thought that was that. However, within one week of my new boss arriving she hand-delivered a sealed envelope to me containing an appropriate reward. The story had been told and action was taken. I have to add that it happened again a few years later and I petitioned in the same way but was told no improvement was coming. I was also overlooked in a reshuffle. However, by then my security and reward lay in my relationship with God and although I still remember the sting, I accept the wound and am at peace.

sometimes you just suffer loss but remain free.

In the cases of being wrongly accused, sometimes I was able to offer my defence which was rarely accepted. At other times it was not in the company's interest for me to offer my defence as I was scapegoated for a failure that affected a major customer. Blaming me somehow kept the company's reputation intact, or at least my boss's reputation. I knew then what a fall guy was. It was hard. It took me a while to find peace. There was some threat to my job. But everything I could do was either not enough or there wasn't anything I could do. Sometimes you just suffer loss but remain free.

so how does it work, powerlessness and self-emptying in employment?

I need here to talk about how we can fulfil the obligation to deliver the services and results we are paid for while realising our powerlessness to actually make it happen. Remember I had 25 years in industry and commence so I've been there. I would say this. Our experience, skill, and preparedness to work hard enable us to make the promises we need to make in as much as they are within our power. On-time delivery, good cost management, valuable quality, promised profitability, a valued and effective service, and a motivated workforce. Whatever your employment is for. However, in the way we go about our work we must realise our powerlessness to actually make it happen. I can't recommend declaring this to your boss particularly. But in reality, anything could happen that could prevent you from achieving your employment goals.

an unintended message carrier.

As we become the poor in spirit, those who realise their powerlessness to make life happen, we are fully released to use all our God-given skills free of the pressure of having to make things happen. We are also open to God giving us ways of working that would previously have been unknown to us before. I've experienced this so many times.

innovative approaches to business and management.

On one occasion, a head office director of the company approached me asking what management books I'd been studying that might explain my innovative approaches to business and management. I hadn't in fact been studying any management books so I ducked the question. Later I was approached again by the same director, so I shared that the book I'd studied and based my everyday life on, was the Message Bible. Some months later the director was returning to head office and I was invited to a leaving gathering. I bought a copy of the Message Bible, hardback, and wrapped it as a gift. I handed the gift over at the gathering in a pub and to my surprise, it was opened there and then. Not sure quite what to expect I waited. The immediate public comment that came was "so this is what he's been reading, I can't wait to give it a try". Two months later I received a message from the director thanking me for the book and that it had been read.

self-emptying the poison

In our powerlessness we will become aware of the things we've allowed into us that are poisoning us, and limiting our capability, and we will be able to self-empty them. Things like my reputation, the need to be seen as successful, and the fear of failure. All these and more need to be self-emptied but only as and when God makes us conscious of them. This is when we become fully responsible or response-able. Able to respond in an effective way to the challenges and opportunities that arise. In my experience, I always knew that the obligations of my employment had to be met. However, the way I met those obligations was the difference between living well and living poorly. I hope I've said enough there.

it's all gift

Personally, in the long run, I found abilities way beyond myself and experienced results way beyond what the job roles demanded. At one stage in my career as the general manager of a business, we were delivering outstanding results and the workforce was happy and committed. So, it was decided I should be moved to other parts of the business to bring results there also. This involved several days of testing held at a luxury hotel of golfing fame. I was getting somewhat carried away thinking, hey, I'm really good at this, I can do anything. The night before the testing began, I had a dream in which I was weeping for a long period of the night. In the dream, God said this is all a gift that came through openness and emptiness. It was never you. It could be removed at any time.

Anyway, the testing went ahead over several days with much fine dining in between as was the way then. The outcome was that I demonstrated none of the skills that could possibly have led to the results achieved in the business. I was ready for this. The managing director said to me that if they had known this, they would never have employed me in that role. However, the financial benefits were so great to the company, and he was convinced in some way it was all coming from me, so he said all we can do is carry on. They couldn't risk removing me from the role.

how does it work in households and families?

In the same way as in employment, we want to do the best for our households and families. You will, sooner or later, realise you really are powerless to make this happen. We must fully accept our calling to do the best for our families and do everything we can. At the same time, the only way we will be able to do everything we can is to realise our powerlessness to make this happen and become open to God. We will then become aware of the hidden drives that poison us and we can self-empty them. I'll say more later about how this works in the family when we talk about the meek.

You can never do enough. There will be many times, and I find most of the time, in life, that everything I can do is never going to be enough to make life happen for me and mine. This is part of the realisation of our powerlessness to make life happen. Strangely enough, the Kingdom of heaven comes bringing peace whatever the circumstances. Often as not, more wisdom comes, and then a way appears where there was no way.

an exercise

I'm assuming you're still practicing the exercise ....

In the circumstances of everyday life, God is working for the good in all things, as I do everything I can while realising my powerlessness to make life happen.

As you practice this, God will reveal to you what you need to begin to self-empty yourself of. It will be something that is poisoning you. It could be something like the life-controlling need to make something specific happen, or an entitlement you feel you have, or a vulnerability you have, or a grievance you have. Please don't go looking for something that might be obvious. You may have many things from my list but you would only want to consider self-emptying the thing you feel empowered and ready to empty out. Self-emptying is also a journey. It will take a while and will take several encounters before you can self-empty something. Be assured though, release is coming.

Sometimes you will find that the thing you have to self-empty was at one time necessary and you might say ....
"I needed you once but now it's time to let you go." I find myself saying, I needed you once and I thank you for that but now I don't need you, you need me, so it's time to say goodbye. I found this particularly true in bringing our children into adulthood. I once needed to instruct them, telling them what to do. It took me quite some time and some difficulty to transition away from this as they entered adult life. The need was still there in me. I had to begin to practice self-emptying as it was beginning to control my ability to relate well to them.

4. OVERCOMING THE THREAT OF LOSS.

We are on our way to the third and final beatitude of the three that Jesus gave as the way to become more like him, someone who lives well in all circumstances. We've always known that Jesus said he is the 'way' to a new kind of life, well here it is. Before we go to the third beatitude I'm going, in this chapter, to share some more thoughts with you around the idea of surrendering our supposed control over our circumstances.

We misguidedly exercise our own power, drawn in by the illusion that we can have control and the lie that we need control. If you're still not wholly with me on this I will be sharing some supporting bible wisdom later. One of the main problems for me in surrendering my control over things is the threat of loss. I find the threat of loss to be overwhelming and a common theme. Here is an example from our house buying experience for your entertainment at my expense.

my house buying journey.

At the time of writing this teaching for a Sunday morning, we were on the third house we had surveyed. It was an expensive process. The first two failed to make it through. You may need to concentrate to keep up. We found a buyer for our house but because we had two purchases fall through, we were now some eight months since we accepted his offer. Now, the guy we were buying off, needed more time as he also had a purchase fall through. So, our buyer was threatening to pull out as this delay was the final straw.

We received the phone call while driving in Norfolk. Now, the roads in Norfolk are difficult to follow and we're on sat nav. When this threatening call came in, the sat nav switched off, so now I'm driving blind with an island approaching, and our third attempt to purchase a house is under threat.

The caller declared that the guy buying our house said, if we don't exchange contracts this week then it's all off. Can you imagine how my psyche was coping with sat nav problems on unfamiliar roads and an apparently unmoveable threat on our house purchase? The poor guy buying our house had been put off two times before by us over eight months and lost his mortgage offer which expired due to the time delay requiring him to re-apply for his mortgage. I was well-practiced by then in *doing everything I can, realising my powerlessness to make things happen*, and trusting that God works for the good in all things. (which doesn't necessarily mean God will make it happen for us).

This had made way for me to self-empty anything I'd allowed in that would debilitate me for this house purchase so I was available for divine intervention. Between negotiating roundabouts with no idea which way was correct and looking for somewhere to pull over, I just spontaneously said to the caller, "we give permission for the guy buying our house to negotiate directly with the guy we're buying off and we will abide with whatever they agree on dates". The caller goes off the phone, the sat nav switched back on and we carried on our journey. My wife declared that it was an amazing spontaneous act of wisdom on my part. Me, I was just open and empty and ready for spontaneous divine input. My normal condition is threat-induced anxiety. Remember that phrase, open and empty.

An hour later the agent calls, we're still in the car in deepest Norfolk and the sat nav goes off again. The agent says they have agreed to a stay of execution of ten more days then they will both commit to exchange or it's all finally off. Perfection.

Sometimes even if you've embraced the moments of powerlessness, you may be called upon to surrender whatever remaining power you think you have.

a week later and another threat of loss.

We are now five days away from the new date of exchanging contracts and the agent phones to say the guy buying our house wants an updated look around the house on Tuesday the day before we exchange contracts. Now on that Tuesday, it was to be a chaotic day in our household. The car was due in the garage for repairs (one of my great vulnerabilities) so no transport. My son and his family and dog were staying with us while they had work done on their house. We're sleeping downstairs in the front room on a mattress on the floor plus we've packed to move so everywhere is cluttered with boxes. So, on the speakerphone, me and my wife said to the agent in chorus, nooooo, he can come in ten days' time when we will be back to normal.

A reaction out of fear and chaos not a response from a place of rest. I thought I'd fully embraced the powerlessness of the situation after responding so well to the threats in the car. But there was still some control over the circumstances I was holding onto and self-emptying was called for. A day later, my wife who is more spiritually prepared for life than me, lead me through this self-emptying by saying, "if it were us buying a house we hadn't seen for eight months we would want one last look before we commit". So, we contacted the agent and said the buyer can come whenever he wants. Self-emptying sometimes requires an action to achieve it.

the way of the world

Now, in the way of the world, allowing the guy to view the house again before he exchanges contracts was a bad move. It could have scuppered everything. But in God's way of living, it was the right thing, a life-giving thing even. Sometimes even if you've embraced the moments of powerlessness, you may be called to surrender whatever remaining control you think you have. At this point I had prepared my teaching for Sunday with this story in it, not knowing the outcome. Would the story be any good if the buyer comes and changes his mind? The story was good because it was authentically, our experience of God in our circumstances whatever the outcome. The agent calls a day later saying our buyer doesn't want to put pressure on us and will wait to look around when we're back to normal and after exchanging contracts. Perfection again. There is a God.

this outcome may not have come about.

We may be tempted to think God's work in us and for us is manifested in the outcomes we feel we need, but this outcome may not have come about. We experienced life in all circumstances in our bodies and minds just after we surrendered whatever control we thought we still had to make this thing happen before the results came in. There is at large the idea that God's power is only manifested in the outcomes in our lives, but in reality, God's power is manifested in authenticity, in the kind of people we are becoming, the way we engage with the issues of everyday life in freedom irrespective of the outcomes. A life-giving experience of the presence and power of God, during a storm of issues, not at the end.

a new way of engaging with everyday life.

Jesus offers this new way of engaging with everyday life to a crowd of ordinary people on the side of a mountain in the sermon on the mount, where he introduces the beatitudes. To remind you and summarise; Jesus is saying, that if we want to live freely and lightly in all circumstances like he does, then we must become like him. (I'll do the bible study later). The first three beatitudes are where Jesus shows us how. Bear in mind Jesus is describing his own path here, he's describing himself.

In summary here are the first two beatitude pathways

<u>Openness </u>to possibilities that do not require our control is achieved by following the first beatitude.

> *Blessed are those who, when the circumstances of everyday life come, do everything they can while realising their powerlessness to make life happen.*

They become the poor in spirit and theirs is the Kingdom of Heaven. (Interpretation mine)

<u>Emptiness,</u> to be free of things that we've allowed into us that poison us, is the second beatitude and is only achieved only after practicing the first beatitude.

> *Blessed are those who walk in the self-emptying of the things that are controlling them for they will be held by God instead of being held by their stuff. (Interpretation mine)*

Remember the word mourn in the beatitude is kenos, which means empty. As I close this chapter, I leave you with those two simple ways, openness, and emptiness, to practice becoming more like Jesus and so more free from the need for control. In the next chapter I will show you biblically how this is the path Jesus took and how he is the poor in spirit and the mourning (self-emptying) one.

5. I SEE YOU.

In this chapter, I aim to reveal what self-emptying looks and feels like from a biblical perspective. Later I will be showing you from the bible how Paul reveals to us that Jesus practiced all three of the beatitudes, just in case you were wondering. Remember Jesus is calling us to become more like him so that we may engage with everyday life as he would if he were us and as a result, we would live freely and lightly in all circumstances. This is his great cause and from it all other things will follow.

the cause of Christ

If you asked people what the cause of Christ is you would get different answers that might include the poor or the 'so-called lost' or social justice, or whatever your passion is. There may well be nothing wrong with any of these but I would like to propose to you that the cause of Christ is one thing; that we would become more like him and as a result live his kind of life living freely and lightly in all circumstances. Authentic lives being the greatest witness of all. All other things would then naturally flow from this including all the individual and varied callings and passions. Seek first the Kingdom and all other things will follow.

what self-emptying looks like in reality.

Imagine you've been invited to a large dinner party with influential people. You may think; people might admire me there, or I could make some good contacts and do some networking, or I'm not really interested in 'so-called' influential people, or I'm not really good enough to be here and likely to be humiliated. I would say that whenever we have any of these thoughts or thoughts like them, we are vulnerable. I speak from experience.

the dinner party

In Luke 7:36-50 NIV. Jesus was invited to such a meal. The people there were influential. Jesus had been invited to the Pharisee's house because he was becoming influential and they thought he posed a threat to the religious order of the day.

The normal routine for inviting guests would be to meet them at the door or the portico, a sort of covered archway, and have their feet bathed and perfumed from the grit, grime, and animal droppings of the dusty streets. Then they would be sat in order of importance, the more important closest to the host. This was a display of local hierarchy for all to see and a place where you got to network with the people as important as you.

Now in Jesus' case, they omitted, on purpose, to wash his feet to make a point of how low he was in the order of importance. It was even worse than that, everybody had their feet washed at least, but not Jesus. He was invited to be revealed as someone of no importance at all. So, his feet were dirty and smelly. A signal to all of his inferiority.

then came the woman

The next thing we note is that Jesus is seen by a woman passing by who knelt at his feet. This means that Jesus was there to be seen by all and didn't even make it past the covered portico into the banquet hall. This is declaring Jesus to be of no importance, to be shamed, ridiculed, and invited in order to be publicly excluded.

The question I ask you is, why wasn't Jesus angry, upset, ashamed, embarrassed, or hurt by this experience? How would you or I feel? I would probably have left but Jesus didn't. To make it worse the woman who stopped and knelt at his dirty feet was a woman of ill repute. We know this because she uncovered her hair in public.

I bet the pharisee couldn't believe his luck as this would have ridiculed Jesus even more in the eyes of his guests and society. This was a public display.

because he was empty

The reason Jesus wasn't angry, upset, ashamed, embarrassed, or hurt was because he had emptied himself of anything that he could be angry about or upset by; ashamed of; embarrassed or hurt by. His life was a walk of self-emptying. Remember the word in the text for his walk was kenosis, self-emptying. His vulnerabilities had been emptied out along with his aspirations, entitlements, pride, ego, and self-esteem. So, when the moment came, he realised his own powerlessness to make things happen, was empty of all that would contaminate his behaviour and as a result, he lived freely and lightly. You have to remember that Jesus ....

Who being in the form of God, did not count equality with God something to be grasped. But he emptied himself, taking on the form of a slave, becoming as human beings are; and being in every way like a human being.

Philippians 2:5-7. The New Jerusalem Bible

I do the short bible study in chapter 11. Jesus emptied himself of all entitlement, to become like us so that we might become like him.

self-esteem

People talk about our self-esteem being too high or too low. I'd like to propose to you that the problem with self-esteem is the word, self. I don't believe we need to address 'so-called' low or high self-esteem. I believe we must empty self-esteem from our lives. When asked by someone what they might give up for lent I said, try giving up self-esteem and at the end of lent, you won't need to pick it up again.

what was Jesus then able to do in this freedom?

Well, the effect of openness and emptiness upon him enabled a woman of ill repute to see him as a person who would accept her unconditionally. She literally saw God in him. We probably wouldn't have seen this as a miracle but it was. Culturally it was impossible for such a woman to behave like this and yet she walked straight up to him and knelt at his feet. She saw God in someone who had surrendered his power to make life happen and become like us so that we might become like him.

The thought here is that as we follow him in walking these beatitudes into our life, then people will see the freedom from God in us, and approach us for the life they see in us even though they don't know what it is.

I see you

Not only did the woman see Jesus but Jesus saw her. At the height of the potential outrage and injury of the way he had been treated, he saw her. He wasn't poisoned by reacting to what had been done to him. He was free to see. As we follow him in openness and emptiness, we too will see how God is working in those we meet in everyday life. I have a dear friend who when approaching people, sees how God is working in their lives and asks them about it. Something I've begun to walk into myself as I walk the beatitudes. It's a true wonder.

Getting back to the account of Jesus at the Pharisee's house. The impact went further in that the woman wept. There was obviously some kind of release being experienced by her. Perhaps a release from the effect of who she had become is inferred. Try not to judge her, as the same is true for us as we see and are seen by God. In this passage she is us, being released from the kind of person we have been becoming.

But there were no prayers said, no interview, nothing of the bible declared over her. Yet here she was weeping at the feet of the one who is the poor in spirit. What I am saying here is that the power of heaven was exchanged between Jesus and the woman, not because he was God incarnate but because he became like us and practiced his chosen powerlessness to make life happen and self-emptied all that would poison his behaviour.

heavens door

Practicing and living these first two beatitudes literally opens heaven's door to us, for us, and through us for another. It opens heaven's door to our experience of living and opens heaven's door to those we live with, our households, our workplaces, our neighbourhood, and our society. As the first beatitude promises.... for theirs is the kingdom of heaven.

How did we miss this? The poor in spirit are not those poor people who need our help, the poor in spirit are those who, in embracing their powerlessness, are becoming free of the need for control. It's less weak and more meek. But I'm jumping ahead to the third beatitude and must return to where we were.

I've experienced this unexpected release of the power of heaven, bringing freedom, many times but didn't see the link with the beatitudes. I'm guessing some of you may also have experienced this or are experiencing it now. Let it come.

an unexpected intimacy.

For the woman, not only did the impact go further but so did the intimacy. She was impacted by the power of heaven, experienced release from who she had become, and wept. But that's not the end of it. She then washed his feet with her tears and dried them with her hair. Oh, my goodness. Remember the Pharisee in effect declared Jesus to be of no honour by refusing to have Jesus' feet washed. This woman however automatically washes his feet with her tears. She had travelled through encounter and release, to worship, and I'm sure she had no idea what she was doing. This was not contrived for effect or reward. I don't think it was even thought about. She just did it.

what does this mean for us?

We can and will travel through encounter and experience a release from who we have become to worship without instruction or understanding, in spite of who we are or how we live. Read that sentence again. Those who see us as the poor in spirit, like how this woman saw Jesus, can and will, through who we are becoming, travel through encounter and release, there will often be tears, and into worship. There will often be no understanding, no expression of faith, no confession or repentance. They all come later empowered automatically by the encounter with Heaven.

The woman should have had her hair covered. To have your hair uncovered was a sign you were of ill repute. It was shameful for a woman to have her hair uncovered in public. This tells us something about the woman. This also tells us the powerful place of being authentically honest about who we are, even when we're not pleased with who we are becoming.

we can only experience the life-giving presence of God in reality.

So, we must not hide from or deny our present reality if we want to meet with God and find freedom as she did. A friend recently described it by saying

> "if we want to find freedom in our circumstances and a way through then we must embrace reality for what it is, no more and no less".

I have found this to be particularly helpful. Instead of trying to sort out what might happen in the future, or try to cover shame or guilt for the past, I am more helped by embracing the present moment for what it is. It can be painful but I find my head clears and I can think clearly and discover ways of thinking that were not previously perceived by me. This is because I can't experience God in the past or the future because although he is there, I'm not there. I can only experience God in the present moment by embracing it for what it is. I'll say more about this later in the chapter about the practice of giving way.

what happened to the shame.

Note what happens to the shame after she is encountered by the one who is poor in spirit. She is so free of shame that she uses her uncovered hair, which represents her shame, to dry Jesus' feet. This means that our guilt or shame are no barrier to an encounter with the power of heaven. I tend to think of these things as being more relevant to other people but the main message has to be for me first. How many times do I feel as though my behaviour has put me out of reach of God's hand, out of reach of his mercy, of his affection towards me, of his healing? The way Jesus and this woman share a heavenly encounter shows me that I too can always, whatever the circumstances, experience the same.

then there was the perfume.

She bathed his feet with perfume. Why would a woman of ill repute, a prostitute, carry perfume? Was it perhaps part of her trade to perfume herself for her clients? But she did what the pharisee failed to do which made her more honoured than him. She perfumed Jesus' feet. Does this reveal that literally everything is redeemed by an encounter with the one who is poor in spirit? Think about that and how far-reaching it is.

hi-fidelity (hi fi)

It would be easy to think that all this applies to a prostitute so how can it apply to me? Well, in the bible the prostitute represents unfaithfulness or infidelity. In my generation, we had something called hi fi. Hi-fidelity. It was a stereo sound system that faithfully reproduced the original music. When we are faithful to the creator in the way we live we could be said to have hi-fidelity. Equally, when we so often live in a way that is not faithful to the creator, we could be said to have low fidelity. So, the woman in the story represents us when we live in low fidelity.

time for an exercise – I see you.

I could go on talking about this encounter for ages and you may see it differently, but the point here is to reveal what the self-emptying (mourning) of the second beatitude looks and feels like from a biblical perspective and in real life. You may want to reflect longer on this event from my notes or from the account in the bible in Luke 7:36-50.

the exercise

Can I encourage you to reflect on this event in this chapter or from the original bible reading, not for understanding or for teaching but for encounter? Read and pause and reflect. Allow the feelings and the emotions to come as you imagine yourself perhaps first as the woman and then as Jesus in this event. Give it a few days to soak in and keep returning to it.

I hope you're beginning to realise the power of simply practicing the first two beatitudes. You may now want to go back and re-read the previous chapters although I do review them in short form in the next chapter.

In the next chapter, I'll take you to the culmination of this walk.

"Blessed are the meek for they will inherit the earth". Matthew 5:5 NIV.

Then I'll show you how all three work together as we walk in them, transforming us to become like Jesus, living his kind of life, living freely and lightly in all circumstances. Jesus said that he came so that we may have life in all its fullness. John 10:10. His life. To have that life we are called to become like him and the first three beatitudes are the path Jesus walks and the path he calls us to walk to become more like him.

But up to now, you've only had the first two beatitudes so it's time, in the next chapter, for me to introduce you to the third.

"Blessed are the meek for they shall inherit the earth".

6. THE MEEK SHALL INHERIT THE EARTH.

Before I lead into the third of what I call the three transformation beatitudes, I need to remind you of the first two in shortened form. Remember the calling is to become like Jesus and as a result, live his kind of life with him. A life that lives well in all circumstances. Jesus is describing himself in these first three transformation beatitudes and invites us to walk the same way. I wonder if this is what Jesus means when he says he is the 'way'.

The first beatitude we are called to walk in is,

As the circumstances of everyday life come, we are to do everything we can while realising our powerlessness to make life happen.

This is the blessed place of openness and in realising our powerlessness we find peace from our need for control by becoming open to the life-transforming power of heaven. We become the poor in spirit just as Jesus did. For theirs is the kingdom of heaven.

The second beatitude we are called to walk in ....
is enabled and empowered by the first one. You just can't walk in the second beatitude in your own power, you need the promised kingdom of heaven from the first. The first opens us, the second empties us. Only once we are open can we be emptied.

Only once we are experiencing the power of heaven will we have the power to see, and self-empty (mourn/kenos), the things we've allowed in that are poisoning our lives.

We will self-empty our self-interests, our entitlements, our fears, our fantasies, our vulnerabilities, and our need often naturally and understandably compulsive need, for us to get things sorted for ourselves and our loved ones. This is the blessed place of emptiness. Are my potatoes really growing under there perhaps I should pull them up, and see?

detachment

I want here to introduce 'detachment' as it occurs in the third beatitude, now that practicing the first two beatitudes has made us ready for it.

My mom was 98 years old and facing the issue of needing 24-hour care. In my nature, my mind runs to how this might work out for her and for me. The 'need to know' clicks in and I'm unsettled until I can work out some kind of certainty. I need this to work out the way I feel I need it to work out. I consider that the rest of the family may have their own versions of how they feel they need it to work out too. The danger is that we can each attach to the outcomes we feel we need. For me, this then affects my behaviour. Do I push for what I feel is needed? Do I just give up fearing I'll not get what I feel is needed? Am I defeated by the worry of it all and just give in?

These are my only options once I've attached myself to the outcomes I believe I need. I attach to my own desired outcomes when I'm neither open nor empty. This is not the case with the meek as recorded in the third beatitude.

Blessed are the meek for they shall inherit the earth. Matt 5:5 NIV

There is the assumption here that I even think I know what is the best outcome. Attachment to outcomes causes us to blindly pursue those outcomes. We have in effect, having attempted to gain control, placed ourselves under their control. This in turn blinds us to reality and remember we can only experience God in authentic reality. Attachment to our own outcomes also drives us into a stream of very unhelpful even hurtful behaviour. I have created my own storm which begins to overwhelm my boat. I can hear Jesus saying to me where is your faith, you don't need to be here. Mark 4:35-41 NIV

it's different for the meek

There are people who are able to engage with the issues of life well, in all circumstances. They are able to live freely and lightly, come what may, and are a pleasure to live around. Jesus is one of them. They inherit the earth according to Jesus. I'll talk about that later. They don't need to push for the outcomes they feel they need and they don't fear not getting them.

This is because they are no longer living with the need for things to work out the way they feel they need them to. They are not living with the illusion that they can have control over their lives or the lie that they need it. They are detached from the outcomes they feel they need so they are not wrestling with the 'need to know' how things will turn out.

It's not because they have no passion, or have given up, or take no responsibility. And it's not because they don't care how things work out or because things aren't important. It's because they are free to live without the 'need to know' how things will work out. They have been prepared by living the first two beatitudes, to avoid attaching themselves to the outcomes they may feel they need, or they are able to detach from those outcomes, should they have become attached. They are living freely and lightly as in Matthew 11:29, living the rhythms of grace. They are 'the meek'.

intimate and courageous engagement

In this detached state they are able to engage intimately and courageously with the circumstances of life without the hindrance of needing certain outcomes or the fear of not getting them. They are able to work hard and effectively all the time free of the 'need to know'. They inherit the earth. They are able to fully play their part and they inherit a way through that may well have been unknown to them, beyond them, and is not of their making. Sometimes I believe that if I can't see a way through then there is no way through. That may sound arrogant but it is born of the 'need to know'. Under this threat, I am overwhelmed and my behaviour is erratic and unhelpful.

the 'need to know' pandemic.

The 'need to know' is pandemic in our humanity like a disease. It may well be the cause of the original sin; the need to know what only God knows. On a lighter note, the 'need to know' is also entertainment. We really enjoy the 'who dun it' programs on tv. Our tv schedules are littered with detective series although I have to say we enjoy the lighter drama ones rather than the very dark versions. It's the same with sport. We watch the tennis, and the pre-match chatter from the commentators is all around the 'need to know' who will win and why. The Jane Austen films tease us with the 'need to know' whether the maiden will win her hero. The news is full of the need for certitude, the 'need to know' the future. Recently the reporter was saying that tomorrow the Queen will give her speech, and then proceeded to tell us what the Queen will say. Why can't we just wait for the Queen?

Humanity is addicted to the 'need to know' that things will work out the way we feel they need to. Are my potatoes really growing under there or shall I dig them up, and see? The consequences on the potatoes are similar to the consequences on our circumstances, not good.

blessed are the meek for they shall inherit the earth.

The meek are those who are content to live without 'the need to know' how things will work out because they are detached from the outcomes.

> *They are* <u>*open*</u> *to things outside of their control, by working passionately and courageously towards a goal, while all the time realising their powerlessness to make things happen,*

> *and they are empty of all the things that may poison and control them on the way.*

It is practicing these two things that prevents them from attaching to their own outcomes, outcomes that would have then controlled them. The meek, therefore, now detached from their outcomes, live freely and lightly as they journey through the circumstances of everyday life as Jesus does. The meek are becoming more like Jesus and intuitively think, speak and act as he would if he were they. Jesus is describing himself as the meek and calling us to become more like him.

Becoming the meek as you now know from the above requires us to live, or walk, 'the way' of the first two beatitudes. The question someone asked me was; to become the meek, is a decision required to detach ourselves from our outcomes for our circumstances. Is detachment a choice we have to make? I'm still pondering this. Certainly, when we don't walk in the first two beatitudes, we have no choice about the attachment to outcomes; we will attach ourselves in some way or other to the outcomes we feel we need in order to gain that illusion of control. Attaching to try to make life happen, attaching through fearing we can't make it happen, or attaching in resignation giving in and giving up. It's in our nature.

the route to attachment

I can now summarise the overall route to attachment to our own outcomes. You will see the pattern of the first three beatitudes here.

We are driven by our need to make things happen, compelled by the things we have allowed in that poison us, like entitlement or hurt, and now held by our attachment to the outcomes we feel we need to gain control over our lives. As long as we hold on to our outcomes, they will hold us.

I repeat, as long as we hold onto our outcomes, they will hold us.

an unexpected experience of release

I was chatting with someone recently about how this is all working out in our experience of everyday living. We had both found ourselves constantly repeating the first beatitude; as the issues of everyday life arise we do everything we can while realising our powerlessness to make things happen. We had both been impacted by the sheer effectiveness of this practice. When something happened that caused a threat or challenge, instead of pressing in and fighting, or giving up and running, we found that just doing everything we can while realising our powerlessness to make things happen, just broke the threat or challenge. The experience of release was unexpected because the compulsion to push in to control things or be overwhelmed by threat, was so strong. It seemed unstoppable in those moments. Yet, pausing and doing everything we can while realising our powerlessness to make things happen, just mysteriously cleared the air. The circumstances could then be engaged with, freely and lightly.

the significance of the first beatitude.

I totally underestimated the significance and efficacy of the first beatitude as practiced above. I would go so far as to say that if we could practice the first beatitude perfectly then we wouldn't need the other two.

Certainly, as we walk in the first two beatitudes, I believe that in some cases we will automatically not have the 'need to know' how things will work out and so not attach to certain outcomes. We will become the meek and live freely. However everyday living is more likely to mean that we will often not walk in the first two beatitudes or not well enough and will find ourselves needing to know how things will work out and we will become attached to certain outcomes that will then control us.

This is certainly the case for me. Sometimes I find myself living freely and detached from outcomes and at other times I find myself attached and compulsive about outcomes. When this happens, I can consciously decide to detach and be free. This usually requires me to go back to the first beatitude and realise my powerlessness and then to the second to self-empty the self-interests that are revealed. But at least I know where to go.

This also assumes I am conscious of my 'need to know' and my attachment to certain outcomes. The unconsciousness usually comes through the struggle for control, or the anxiety, or the poor behaviour, created by my attachment to outcomes. But I do eventually become conscious as I walk the beatitudes. I guess walking the first two beatitudes perfectly, we would never need the third. Think about it. That's never going to happen this side of eternity.

engaging or attaching

There is a clear difference between attaching to the issues of our lives and engaging with them.

We attach through the 'need to know', born of the drive to

make life happen and compelled by our self-interests or perceived needs. The need for control.

Alternatively, engaging with the issues of everyday life is when we find ourselves sufficiently detached from the outcomes that we are able to see how we can participate freely.

This I find often leads to a much more loving and effective engagement. I can draw closer to the issues because I'm not fear-driven by my need for control. I discern new ways of thinking (the mind of Christ), and new ways of speaking and acting. I am much more compassionate and full of wisdom. I see ways through, that I couldn't see before, and often experience outcomes I didn't think were possible. The blessing though overall is not so much in the outcomes but in the new kind of life experienced as we journey through everyday life.

As Jesus says, the meek shall inherit the earth. Inherit a kind of life on earth that is truly, life in all its fullness, whatever the circumstances or the outcomes.

so, do I attach to the issues of life or engage with them

This is really important to me. I care. I want to play my part but I realise I must not become attached to my own outcomes, by needing to know how things will work out. I could summarise it by a need for certainty. Certainty is, however, an illusion as revealed by the covid pandemic of 2020/21 and ongoing as I write.

an example of detachment from my life - the car damage

A guy ran into our car while it was parked. The neighbour heard the bang and went to the window to see that a van had backed into our car, while he was turning around. The driver had pulled up, blocking the road, to inspect the damage. He then drove off, but the neighbour got his registration number.

I contacted the police who said it was an open and shut case, as it was an offence to drive away from an accident causing damage. They said the insurance claim should be straightforward. You're already guessing where this is going. The police contacted the driver, through his registration number, and he admitted the incident but said on inspection he saw no damage. So, the police said the offence of not reporting it could be waived on the basis that he was being honest.

My insurance company was fully briefed, but the driver's insurance company said he had no recollection of the event and wasn't there. On my declaring the neighbour as a witness, the driver's insurance company said they wouldn't accept that, as the neighbour couldn't be impartial. Even though the neighbour had seen it all, we had the damage, and the driver had admitted being there, to the police.

I'm guessing you might be a little exasperated. I certainly was. The car was nearly new but the damage didn't prevent us from driving it. A large dent in the wing and door not quite breaking the door seal thankfully. I began to realise, that although I was entitled to a repair on the other guy's insurance, it may not be coming.

My powerlessness to make this happen was becoming clear and I began to self-empty my self-interest, my entitlement to a repair. However, I continued to work towards achieving a repair but I was no longer attached to this as the outcome. I contacted the police and told them the story. They said they were satisfied with the neighbour's witness and clearly the driver of the van had misled us. Apparently, because the driver lied to the insurance company, I could have pushed for a prosecution which in turn would have tipped the insurance into my favour. However, the other driver was a builder, and a prosecution would have damaged his business, played havoc with future insurance, and given him a criminal record.

In my new state of peace, with a clear mind and a clean heart, I decided that someone had to do the right thing, so I let it go. In effect, I automatically released myself from the issue. Every time I look at that dent, I remember mercy. I managed to engage with the issue without attaching myself to the outcome I wanted.

a 'way' of living

Jesus' calling on our lives, is to become more like him. We will then think his thoughts speak his words and do what he would do. We will live freely and lightly as he says in Mathew. This kind of living is why Jesus came so that we would experience life in all its fullness in all circumstances. John 10:10

For those of us who think about ministry or witness, be assured that when we seek the Kingdom of Heaven in this way, then everything else will follow. Our everyday lives become the witness and the impact on those around us, the ministry.

the calling to become like him - in summary

As the issues of everyday come, we are called to do everything we can, whilst realising our powerlessness to make life happen. We become the poor in spirit like Jesus and experience the Kingdom of heaven. This place is called the blessed place of openness. (first beatitude)

Then, we will become aware of the things we've allowed in, that are controlling us; entitlements; self-interest; the need to make things happen that we feel need to happen, for us and our households. These things make us vulnerable, and being full of them, there is no room for the better way God has for us. So, we are called to self-empty them (mourn: kenos: empty) as God makes us aware of what they are. The power to see these things and the power to self-empty them comes from living the first beatitude; for theirs is the Kingdom of Heaven.

As we self-empty we are blessed, as we are no longer held captive by these things, and instead are held by the father. For they shall be comforted. (second beatitude). This is called the blessed place of emptiness.

Finally, as we live the first two beatitudes and become open and empty, we will be able to see where we have attached ourselves to specific outcomes, compelled by the 'need to know' how things will work out. We will be freed from the 'need to know' and so detached from the outcomes we feel we need. We become the meek. Detached from our outcomes we will be released to play our part fully, in ways we may never have expected. Remember, God is working for the good in all things. This is what we are now participating in, the way God is working for the good in our circumstances, where ever it takes us. We become the meek, like Jesus; blessed are the meek for they shall inherit the earth. (third beatitude)

open, empty and detached

We become open, empty, and detached. Now we can live freely and lightly in all circumstances.

7. WHAT DOES TRANSFORMATION LOOK LIKE IN EVERYDAY LIFE

The first three beatitudes, I have called, the transformational beatitudes. The following beatitudes are the effects of living the first three. I'm now going to include the fourth, seeking righteousness; the fifth, the merciful; the sixth, the pure in heart; the seventh, the peacemakers; and the eighth, the walk of righteousness. This is what transformation looks like in everyday life.

disillusioned by apparent failure

Before I start to share about these, I need to say again that they are the effects of walking in the first three beatitudes of *openness, emptiness, and detachment.*

Remember, openness is about realising powerlessness, emptiness is about emptying self-interest, and detachment is about detaching from our own outcomes.

The reason I need to repeat this is because somehow or other we have believed that we must just try harder to become the righteous, the merciful, the pure in heart, and the peacemakers. You must have discovered by now, that it's impossible to just try to become these things, or even understand what they really are. I fear that many of us will have become disillusioned by this apparent failure.

These things are the effects; the fruit on the tree. So, you can't just try harder to create an apple or be righteous, merciful, pure in heart, or peace-making. What Jesus is saying to these simple folk, on the side of a hill, is that this is what life looks like when we walk in and live *openness, emptiness, and detachment*. Remember, it's all about becoming more like him.

I hope this will burst the bubble of trying harder to do something we could never do, be something we could never be, just by trying. Now we are free to set our hearts on becoming more like him.

All I need to do now is to decode the following beatitudes, so we can see them clearly in our everyday lives, and know it's the life of God in us. This I believe, leads us to realise the depth of intimacy we can experience in this shared life with God.

a time for tidying up many strands

This chapter presents a time for tidying up many strands of thought. The chapter will be longer, although segmented by subheadings covering those strands of thought, so you can navigate through it and return to the things that cause you to reflect deeper. I'll start with the fourth beatitude and then head into the additional areas for reflection.

hungering and thirsting for righteousness, the fourth beatitude

Matthew 5:6-16 NIV

> *Blessed are those who hunger and thirst for righteousness for they will be filled.*

Remember righteousness is an effect of living the first three beatitudes, so we're not trying to be righteous, we're looking for the signs of it in our days. Righteousness in the Old Testament, which Jesus would have been referring to, meant the very presence of God. So, it's got nothing to do with trying to do the right thing. Eugene Peterson has it clearly in his version in the message.

Matthew 5:6-16 MSG

> *You're blessed when you've worked up a good appetite for God.*
> *He's food and drink in the best meal you'll ever eat.*

So, we're not hungering and thirsting, working up a good appetite, to be able to do the right thing; not that kind of false righteousness. It's impossible to do the right thing consistently, by trying. We're hungering and thirsting to experience the very presence of God, undistracted by us trying to make life happen or by trying to be righteous. Which by the way is what God wants too, to experience our very presence. So, it's about experiencing the intimacy of the presence of God in our everyday moments, and God experiencing us in those moments. Remember the intimate, mutual, 'I see you' just like in the film Avatar?

Note also, that this is the first effect of becoming more like Jesus, and it will come automatically without trying or earning, but as an outflow of living the first three beatitudes. It's the most important thing for us, and for God. Isn't that great? Before anything we may think, say, or do, God wants for us to experience his presence, and for him to experience our presence. Jesus said that they will be filled with God's presence, his very life. Righteousness.

the simple way

The people on the side of that mountain 2000 years ago, understood the simple things, like a flask of oil or wine with a stopper in it. So, in talking about openness and emptiness, Jesus was possibly alluding to a flask with a stopper in it, as an easy-to-understand version of our everyday lives, when talking about being filled. He had just explained to them, how to become, this open and empty bottle, in the first two beatitudes, remember? Being filled can only happen if the bottle of our lives is first open;

it can only be filled if it is empty; and it can only be filled with new wine when it has become detached from being refilled with what was in it before. Ring any bells? (the first three beatitudes, *open, empty, and detached*).

So, Jesus wasn't being cryptic, talking about the poor in spirit/powerless/*open*; those who mourn/kenos/*empty*; and the meek/*detached*. He was possibly talking about a flask *being open, empty, and detached*. They would have seen this easily, although we may not have. You might say it got lost in translation.

walking the beatitudes path instead of trying.

Openness occurs when we realise our powerlessness to make life happen and become the poor in spirit who receive the power of heaven for our daily lives. (the first beatitude).

Emptiness occurs as heaven's power shows us what we have in us, that makes us vulnerable; like the compulsion of self-interest, entitlement, or just the sheer need to make things alright for us and ours. I believe that once the spirit reveals to us what is poisoning us, we will automatically self-empty/mourn it. (second beatitude).

Once open and empty, we are equipped to detach from the outcomes we previously thought we needed, in favour of how God will be working, and become the meek like Jesus. (third beatitude).

I hope you don't mind me repeating this three-fold pathway of *open, empty, and detached*. It's because it's absolutely essential that you get this and begin to live it.

So, Jesus is saying that you can only be filled with a life for all circumstances, experiencing the presence of God (righteousness), once you become *open, empty, and detached*. And, walking in this way is the way we hunger and thirst for it, not by trying harder.

but the way I see things is the way they really are.

I'm not naturally open to my own powerlessness to make life happen. The problem is, that the way I see the things of everyday life, is the way I believe they really are. I'm subconsciously convinced of this, as I believe we all may be.

So, the best journey route for going on holiday is the route I find. I'm convinced of it, and I'm closed to any other possibility. I hold onto and defend my version, to prevent things from going out of my control, which I believe is then out of control. I'm driven by the need to make a smooth journey Self-interest.

But I am part of a family unit who have other requirements for this journey, like a toilet stop, or a stop off at a beauty spot. As these things pile up, I experience anxiety that the whole journey will fragment out of my control.

You see, I believe that I must make this journey happen and that it can, and must, be under my control. But a moment of reflection would reveal, that I can't control traffic jams, accidents, or breakdowns. So, in my belief that I can make this thing happen, how vulnerable am I, when and if, any of these things occur? I am closed.

the compulsive need to be in control

You might think this is a trivial example, but for me, it's not only true but can be typical of the way I live my days. I also believe that in some way it's typical for everyone. Imagine this way of living in conversation with people; in a place of work; or in the way I relate to those close to me. The compulsive need to gain control over what's happening. The problem is that it's a blind spot so you can't see it, and I can't convince you of it. I'm hoping that God will raise your consciousness of it, through these pages.

Being closed at any level, and in any circumstance, means we are not hungering and thirsting for a way forward, other than one we can control. I believe these other ways forward, come from experiencing the presence of God, whether we acknowledge it's God or not. Some people call it a spiritual way or a mystical way. I have no problem with that.

For this other way, we need to be open to the possibility that we are powerless to make life happen, the way we see it happening. My reaction to a traffic jam would immediately betray my futile attempt at control over a holiday journey.

So, in this chapter, I've relieved us of the idea, that we need to try harder to be righteous enough to be able to think, speak, and do the right thing. Because righteousness here is experiencing the presence of God, which will enable us to do the very best thing. And I've revealed, that experiencing the presence of God is the first and primary effect of walking in the first three beatitudes of *open, empty, and detached*. I've also, clumsily probably, tried to show us how we can live naturally closed, in the circumstances of everyday life, denying ourselves the promised kingdom of heaven power we need in our lives.

Jesus said who touched me – as power went out from him Luke 8:45 NIV

heaven's door.

I believe that every time we realise/embrace our powerlessness to make life happen, Jesus says "who touched me" as he felt power go out from him. Power from him to us. Power for what. My guess is that we tend to think of God's power for fixing things, making things happen, or achieving the particular outcome we want.

But it's less a case of power for this or that outcome, as I shared in my car damage story, and more, the power of an ongoing intimate experience of the presence of God which will transform us into his likeness enabling us to live life in all its fullness in all circumstances. These are life-changing moments flowing throughout the days of our everyday lives. They literally open heaven's door to the circumstances we find ourselves in. They open heaven's door to our households, our families, our friendships and fellowships, our employment, our community, and society. They give us life and sow the seeds of God's life everywhere. Could there be anything more central than becoming more like Jesus in this way?

power works both ways

Sadly, when we deny ourselves and our households the presence and power of God by being closed, we are held not by God, but by the outcomes we are holding on to.What we hold on to holds us.

We in effect give the things we are holding out for, power over us. They can determine our behaviour, our values, and our sensitivities. Holding out for the outcomes we want invariably defeats what we were looking to produce in the first place.

We were watching an episode of Downton Abbey again recently, a long-running tv show. The Earl had believed he could secure the future of the Downton Abbey Estate by investing practically all of their wealth in the sure bet of railway construction after the first world war. He believed beyond the shadow of a doubt that he could make life happen in this way. Remember believing we can, and must, make life happen blinds us. This is the opposite of doing everything we can whilst realising our powerlessness to make life happen.

He is closed. Closed to God and closed to anything or anyone who might get in his way. The venture fails and he loses everything. But he is still closed. His behavioural values change. He becomes insensitive, domineering, and above all fearful. He is still closed and now firmly under the control of the shame of the failure. He attempted to exercise the power of creating financial certainty and held onto his entitlement for that certainty, even though it was lost. Holding onto his entitlement to have succeeded in his investment, poisoned his behaviour and gave it power over him.

He strayed into unfaithfulness to his wife but pulled back just in time. It's only when his wife, whose fortune it was anyway, gives way to the Earl in his failure and embraces him, that he finally becomes open. She is God rescuing him in those moments although she wouldn't have perceived it. I believe that even if his investment had succeeded, he would still be under the power of believing he could create financial certainty. It would control him, making him proud and arrogant about his business. Eventually, it would have broken him, it was just a matter of time.

a sign that we are under the power of something we are holding out for.

In the same way, when we feel people, organisations or circumstances are against us, in our way, stopping us from achieving what we believe we should achieve, it's a sign that we are under the power of something we are holding out for. We have given it control over us. Perhaps a specific outcome. Something we believe we are entitled to. The trespass is that we believe we can, and must, gain sufficient control to make something happen. It may well be an honourable thing or something we really need. But taking this make-it-happen path, we are closed to God, closed to other possibilities, and driven by zeal or fear. I've seen this in industry, commerce, politics, and very sadly in some people who profess faith in God. Starting with me.

when nothing can be in our way.

When we take God's 'way' by being *open, empty, and detached* as Jesus invites us to, there is never anyone or anything in our way, because it's not our way we're taking, it's God's way. As a pastor and business manager, I experienced those who behaved as though people or circumstances, or organisations were in their way. I have done it myself and may still yet do it. The behaviour of the person betrays the motive of trying to gain control. Insensitive, uncaring, looking for the inside track or the best network, instead of valuing all people as God does. Every time I saw it or experienced it myself, I knew almost immediately that it was our own way that was being stood against. More of this world, than in it. Perhaps when we sense anyone or anything is in our way, it's a signal that we're looking to control things and time to reconsider and practice *openness, emptiness, and detachment.*

The remedy then is simple if we will take it. Rather than pushing to try to make things happen, we can surrender our way, by realising our powerlessness to make it happen; self-empty whatever self-interest we've allowed in that is driving us, and so be able to detach from the outcomes we were pushing for. This would be practicing the transformational beatitudes. It ends the trespass of being somewhere we shouldn't; the place of trying to make life happen. Forgive us our trespasses.

revealing the trap.

I had to share the negative side of not being open to God and his ways because I sense that we spend so much of our lives there. Often it begins with a sensible, responsible Christian thing to do. Sadly, if there is a vested interest in there or just the sheer need to get through by any means, then we are inadvertently closed to God however many times we say his name.

I mention this not as a judgement or criticism but to reveal the trap. We must remember that we can't walk in God's ways by just trying to impossibly remember what Jesus would do and then try harder to do that. We walk in his ways by becoming more like him. This is why Jesus' message of the beatitudes is so central. Living the beatitudes transforms us to become more like him and as a result, walks us into a whole new way of living. The Jesus way. He is the way. That's why we are called above all things to become more like him by walking the beatitudes and inherit the Kingdom of heaven on earth. Seek first this way and everything else will be added unto you. Ring any bells?

powers, what we hold on to holds us.

I mentioned earlier about powers. In the bible powers are the things we give power to that will rule us harshly. Powers are most often exampled by money or sex or substance abuse. But anything we allow into us in order to secure the outcomes we feel we need, will become empowered and will hold us prisoner. What we hold onto holds us. Even if we're just holding out for more of what we believe we're entitled to in a relationship, or in employment, or whatever, we will then inadvertently have given that thing power over us and it will drive us into trouble. Trouble like behavioural breakdown, addiction, rage, obsession, or compulsion. You get the idea.

In this beatitude, Jesus calls us to hunger and thirst for righteousness, which we have now discovered means the presence of God. As we hunger and thirst for the presence of God in our days by walking in *openness, emptiness, and detachment*, we will be filled with the outcomes in life's circumstances that are for the good. God works for the good in all things. Romans 8:28. These things totally surpass anything we were holding out for which invariably are the wrong things.

Anything else that we hunger and thirst for will exercise power over us. We might hunger and thirst for fairness, justice, security, certainty, perhaps for a political party, a career or for a person. We might hunger and thirst for our family; the best medical treatment, education, a life partner, or a livelihood. Many of these things are good but if we hunger and thirst for them, we will have no appetite for the presence of God and the resultant working of good into our circumstances.

I experience this so often in myself and in people generally. It is the unacknowledged elephant in the room. The only way we can engage with any of these things well is by thirsting after the presence of God by following Jesus' call to practice *openness, emptiness, and detachment* in all circumstances. Seek first the kingdom then all other things will follow. Remember in the Kingdom of God, God works for the good in all things.

cares.

There is an invisible line between rightly presenting all your cares to God and wrongly hungering and thirsting for them. This is where the things we care about can just become the cares of this world, which will control us. We may not know we have crossed this line until the symptoms appear. Anger, fear, resentment, scheming, undermining, entitlement, compulsion, obsession, zeal. Now if we're reasonably self-aware we will hear these symptoms screaming at us and pull back. But sadly, this pathway blinds us and deafens us so we tend to keep going until there is some kind of crash. A relationship breakdown, a split, a psychological or health breakdown, a sense of defeat.

the end of our rope.

When we reach the end of our rope, as Eugene Peterson puts it in the first beatitude, we will realise our powerlessness to make life happen and become the poor in spirit. This begins again the walk of the three transformational beatitudes where Jesus calls us to become like him. God never gives up on us and we will walk this path over and over again, either by wisdom or by repeatedly reaching the end of our rope. Sadly, we can hold out for years or for much of our lives with the illusion that we can and really must make life happen. It's as though God is relying on us, which may be a definition of zeal, rather than realising that we are relying on God.

I appreciate that you may strongly disagree with me about these things and I want to give you permission to believe what you believe the way you believe it. Perhaps you might be able to extend that same permission to me and read on.

8. BLESSED ARE THE MERCIFUL FOR THEY WILL BE SHOWN MERCY.

May I remind you that living the first three beatitudes transforms us to become more like Jesus, and the following beatitudes are the effects. So, if being merciful is an effect, there is no point in trying to be merciful, you just can't do it. Being merciful is the effect of living the first three beatitudes of *openness, emptiness, and detachment.*

de-coding the text.

I need to de-code the text a little for us to be able to see it as simply as it was said by Jesus to this crowd of everyday people on the side of a mountain. I'll get there as simply as I can.

The word translated as mercy is eleeo, which means to show compassion. The merciful then are those who are able to show compassion. A nice easy start.

It's also more of an active word, so the merciful actually do something, they are able to give compassionate responses as they go about their everyday lives. The word mercy also tries to pick up some of the original meaning. It takes in, the word mere, which was the Roman term for the flow of exchange in the economy. So, we get the word <u>mer</u>chant from it and the word com<u>mer</u>ce.

So, Jesus was in effect saying to these people, that this exchange of compassion was already going on, like the commerce of their everyday lives. It is a continuous cycle or flow of compassion that is coming from and returning to God whether we join in with it or not.

an easy version of mercy.

So, an easy read version of this beatitude would be; blessed are those who step into the continuous flow of compassion coming from and returning to God. They will automatically receive and show compassion. An even simpler version may well be; blessed are the mercy-full for as they outpour it so they will receive more. Those guys on the side of that mountain would have received the easy simple version, possibly from my original example of their understanding of a vessel or flask being *open, empty, and detached* from its original source of filling. So the flask now open and empty can be refilled, not with what it had before, but with the ability to show compassion.

They would have used the emptying and filling of flasks as part of their commerce in wine and oil. So, they would quickly understand that the flask of their lives, once open and empty, could then be filled with compassion, which would be outpoured and replaced by more.

we are not compassion generators.

So why did I take you the long way round? Firstly, to get rid of the idea that Jesus could be saying that I must somehow generate compassion from within myself by doing something before he will show me compassion. It's got nothing to do with what we can generate. God fills the flask assuming we are *open, empty, and detached* from our own filling, and as we out-pour it so he refills it. Simple.

So, when something happens and I feel guilty because I don't feel compassion, I would not then try to feel compassionate as an obligation, or do something out of guilt to show to myself or others, that I am compassionate. Instead, to follow the way Jesus is giving, I would turn my attention to practicing being *open, empty, and detached.* (I'm assuming I can use these terms because you've read the earlier passages and are learning how to live this).

Remember this beatitude about compassion/mercy is spoken only seconds after Jesus calls them to be open, empty, and detached from their versions of life with all their vested interests. They would have been immediately aware, that the way to get into this constant flow of compassion, coming from and returning to God, was *openness, emptiness, and detachment.* So, it's time to become simple folk like those on the mountainside that day.

open, empty, and detached refresher.

Shall I save you having to look back into the previous chapters and remind you? If you are clearly living the first three beatitudes by now you could skip the next three paragraphs. However, every time I write them down in this book I experience a further revelation about myself and a deeper breakthrough. Here they are again.

Openness occurs when we realise our powerlessness to make life happen and become the poor in spirit, who are free from needing to make life happen and receive the power of heaven for our daily lives. (the first beatitude).

Emptiness occurs as heaven's power shows us what we have allowed into us that makes us vulnerable. Like the compulsion of self-interest, entitlement, or just the sheer need to make things alright for us and ours. I believe that once the spirit reveals to us what is poisoning us, we will automatically self-empty/mourn it/kenos. (the second beatitude).

Once open and empty, we are equipped to detach from the outcomes we previously thought we needed, that we had given the power to control us. As a result, we will then be able to see how God will be working for the good in our circumstances and become the meek like Jesus. (third beatitude).

true or false compassion

How do we know if the compassion we may be showing is true and not of our own making? I'm talking about this because it's so easy for us to make the showing of compassion a personal goal or even a ministry because it's the right thing to do. It is not an obligation for Christians to show compassion, which would be completely opposite to the way Jesus shows it, as an automatic outflow.

when compassion is true.

I would say that we know that compassion is true when we have absolutely no vested interest in it. Vested interest can be innocent; like to prove to myself that I can show compassion, or even to show to others that God is compassionate. It can also be less than innocent, yet still hidden from us; like to prove to others that I can show compassion or to satisfy a cause I may have inadvertently created; a cause to show compassion. We may even believe wholeheartedly that Christians, or the Church, should be seen as compassionate so let's get on with making it happen. I always see a red warning flag when the words, should or ought are used. I'm hoping that this far into the journey of the beatitudes you can now see that this would be misguided and man-made. Not that I haven't tried it with the best of intentions.

Compassion is only true when it is divine. It's divine when it flows automatically through a life that is becoming more like Jesus. We now know how Jesus calls us to become more like him, in the first three transformational beatitudes. Become *open, empty, and detached.*

9. GIVE ME AN UNDIVIDED HEART THAT I MAY WALK IN YOUR WAYS.

Blessed are the pure I heart for they will see God. Matthew 5:8-12.

Remember, the beatitudes following the first three transformational beatitudes, are the effects of those first three. You don't have to do them; you are becoming them. *Open, empty, and detached.* Jesus is now showing the people on the hillside what it looks like to walk in the first three beatitudes, that he has just shared with them only minutes before.

In the interest of simplicity, I'll tell you the decode first and then walk you there. You might be wondering about my use of the word decode. I'm just returning us to the simple meaning from Jesus. I'm not a scholar. The original meanings are easy to discover if you look long enough. Sadly, in its enthusiasm and zeal, some of the church may have made these things, duties or obligations or the things we should do in order to validate our faith. Nothing could be further from the truth.

the decode for this beatitude, blessed are the pure in heart for they will see God.

The pure in heart here, are those who do not have a divided heart. It will become obvious as I reveal below. Western Christianity may generally see the pure in heart as an issue of moral purity. I guess we may see purity as applying to things like sexual morality, telling lies, not undermining people, or engaging in contrived behaviour or gossip. The problem here is that the list is endless and everybody probably has their own idea of what is acceptable and what isn't. Thank goodness this beatitude is not about moral purity.

not a mixture of several things

Purity, as used here, comes from the word Kath-ar-os. Meaning not a mixture of several things or not contaminated by other things. Like purified gold, or purified water. Here again, we see Jesus using words from their ordinary everyday lives. The purity of oil in a flask, which they would have easily understood. So, when Jesus used the word translated here as pure, they would have heard uncontaminated, one pure thing. Possibly still thinking of their lives being like a flask of pure oil. And when Jesus said the pure in heart, they would have easily understood it meaning an undivided; a heart not divided by containing many competing things. They would have also known Psalm 86 which says, give me an undivided heart.

So, the pure in heart are those who seek the one thing above all others; the life of God in our lives by becoming more like him, as opposed to seeking the many things they might try to make happen. The many things could be well-meaning things like wanting the best for us and ours, or just seeking the many things of this world first. Either way seeking the many things of a divided heart first, will prevent us from becoming more like him, and prevent us from engaging with anything well. As we become more like him, we will be able to engage well, with the many things be they what you might call Christian things or just anything we choose to engage with, in everyday life. Then there is no divide between sacred and secular, and we can enjoy every sphere of life in the world we live in. You can enjoy your modern pleasures as much as you enjoy Christian fellowship. Or if you like, seek first the Kingdom of God and all the other things will follow.

I will see God

The great treasure of the undivided heart is that I will see God. I love this beatitude. Jesus is telling me that if I walk in the first three beatitudes and become more like him, I will see God. See God in my circumstances, see God in my experience of being alive in everyday life, see God in my relationships, see God in my work, my household, my community, society, and see God in the many pleasures of life I am now free to enjoy. A wonder. I will see God in the TV programs and films I watch. In my teaching times, I often use how I've seen God in films. Or I simply enjoy the films and know that the pleasure is God's gift. We can see God in the beauty and intimacy of a 'til death do us part' partner, forsaking all others. We can see God in the daily encounters we have with people in our everyday lives, and see how God is working for us in our employment. Not so we can add it to some sort of witness we believe we are obliged to share, but just to see and know that God is working for the good in our lives. The impact on those around us will be significant in its own right.

seeing God in employment

In my years of employment in industry and commerce I really enjoyed seeing how God was working in me, for me, and through me. It's so sad in my mind when God is clearly working for us and we can't see it, whether we declare a faith in God or not. The people around me at work often stepped into the empty space created by me, not giving them what Eugene Peterson calls, God-talk. I was clearly experiencing something they became aware of even if it was subconsciously.

I remember one guy, a young manager who worked for me. There were times when, in reshuffles, he worked for other business managers. He approached me one day saying "when I work for you I do really well and prosper but when I work for the other managers I struggle and fail and get into trouble. I got this frequently from those who worked for me. He knew of my faith and was clearly alluding to some sort of benefit to him.

On another occasion, the same guy was being subjected to very difficult circumstances in his marriage. He was about to make a serious mistake himself in retaliation when he literally felt a restraining hand stopping him. In the end, he was telling me that it was God working in him. Remember this is someone who wouldn't declare a faith in God in a Christian sense.

I had another guy who knew, that I knew, he was cheating on his wife. I waited and waited. One day he came into my office unprompted and told me he had taken his wife and family to church that weekend and thought I'd like to know. I could see God working in him, it just took a while, and no condemnation from me.

now you see him, now you don't

I have more stories but the message is, that when we are able to see God, then people see God is us and it's only a matter of time, just like the woman who saw God in Jesus and washed his feet with her tears. God works for the good in all things but we often can't see it. We can't see God. I will always need to do everything I can do in life, but as I hold on to the need to make life happen myself, instead of embracing my powerlessness, I will have a divided heart and as a result, I will not see God. As I fill up with my entitlements, my self-interest, or just the sheer need for things to be sorted for me and mine, I will not see God. And as I remain attached to things needing to work out the way I need them to, guess what, I will not see God. It's a lonely struggle through life when we can't see God working in us, for us, and through us.

I've just illustrated the first three beatitudes again, did you notice. However, as I engage with them, I see God working in my pleasures, my struggles, my hopes and dreams, the threats, and my fears. I also see God working in the lives of those around me where they may not see God at all. I will sometimes say that I see God in what's happening or better still ask them if they can see that God is clearly at work in their circumstances. I've found this to be particularly interesting with those who may not profess faith the way I do and yet are open to see God in their circumstances sometimes resulting in them being encountered and changed. Like the guys I met at work.

you can't just jump into seeing God

Seeing and experiencing God is an effect of walking the first three beatitudes, so you just can't decide you're going to be pure in heart and expect to see God. Why would I even want to see God working, for some kind of advantage, without the intimacy Jesus describes in Matthew … *walk with me, work with me, I'll show you how to live freely and lightly.*

It's a bit like learning to drive. You apply for your provisional licence, then learn some theory, then take some driving lessons, then take a driving test. Then you take some more lessons and take another test until you become more like a car driver. You can then apply for your full licence. Try avoiding all that and just jump into a car and drive it. You would just keep crashing every time you repeated it, which may well describe the way we sometimes live our lives. Just keep crashing.

not something extra for us to do

Practicing the beatitudes, or as some call it, the way of blessing, isn't arduous. It isn't something extra you need to do. Few of us have the time for something extra to do. It's more about the way you approach the things you do. *Open, empty and detached*, and by now it will be more automatic. It soon becomes a simple way of living that quickly gives you new life, and multiplies like loaves and fishes. I wonder if this is what that was all about. Surrendering what we have for what he has for us.

so how is my heart divided

When I'm driving my car, if I'm adjusting my sat nav or the radio or even thinking about what's happening on my phone, then my heart is divided. I'm not seeking first the kingdom of driving well. The consequence of erratic driving is affecting me and others, with potentially serious implications. In the same way, as I go about everyday life, if I'm letting in every fragment of thought into my mind and trying to work through it all on my own, then I live erratically. I react poorly to what's going on because my heart is divided. It affects me and those around me.

Equally, when I allow my heart to become full of issues about my car, my kids, my house, my health, my money or even the issues of society then my heart is divided. According to Jesus, I'm blinded by the unintended but self-inflicted chaos. The underlying problem is that I allow these issues into my mind because subconsciously I believe I am on my own and I must sort them all out. But I am not on my own and I don't need to sort all these things.

They may well all need to be attended to, but not from the scary starting point that it's only down to what I can do.
In this state of self-inflicted chaos, I live a fragmented life switching from one thing to another, leaving fragments of unresolved issues everywhere. It's a very poor way to live and I find myself constantly under the threat of, what if.

The good news is that Jesus is saying I don't need to live like this. I could instead do everything I can while realising my powerlessness to make life happen. I become the poor in spirit and open to participate in ways that are not, me trying to make things happen. It becomes clear then, what I have allowed into my heart that is poisoning me and I can and will self-empty it. It's usually a vulnerability like the threat of loss for me and mine. Now open and empty, I can see the outcomes I'm attached to, as the previously, only acceptable and absolutely necessary ones. I'm attached to these outcomes and have allowed myself to be driven by them. I have empowered them to have control over me. What I hold on to, will hold me.

However, having practiced openness and emptiness, I am able to see God, to see how God is working for me. I can detach from the outcomes I was being driven by and become free to engage with the issues, freely and lightly, wherever they go. My divided heart becomes an undivided heart. I become the pure in heart; *blessed are the pure in heart for they will see God.* And I really, really love seeing God in the moments of my ordinary everyday life, which then become extraordinary moments.

10. THE PEACE-MAKING CHILDREN OF GOD

Blessed are the peacemakers for they will be called the children of God.
Matthew 5:9 NIV

T he key to this beatitude is; 'they will be called the children of God'. Children bear the likeness of their parents, so here Jesus is repeating the call to become more like him.

we are born in the image of God, but
transformed into his likeness.

Jesus is the exact representation of God. (Hebrews 1:3 NIV). According to Jesus, we can become so much like him that we will be called the children of God. This reiterates the fact that Jesus is not expecting us to try to think his thoughts, speak his words and do what he would do. Instead, he is saying, just become more and more like me and you will automatically live like I do, freely and lightly as he says in Matthew 11:28-30 MSG. This is the easy yoke.

Remember Jesus is talking about us being called the children of God, just minutes after telling us how we become them, in the first three beatitudes *of openness, emptiness, and detachment.* The beatitudes following the first three are clearly the effects of the first three not a separate set of impossible instructions. How did we miss that?

When I say, in becoming more like Jesus, we will automatically think his thoughts, speak his words, and do what he would do, try not to think ministry or mission. Try to think less about what you can do for God and more about what God is doing for you, as Eugene Peterson says. A personal transformation. Think more along the lines of, this is how I will engage with the circumstances of everyday life, this is the sort of person I am becoming. Living well in all circumstances, living freely and lightly.

Ministry or mission or whatever you call the impact on the world around us that God administers through us will be an automatic, innocent, uncontrived outflow as we become more and more like Jesus. Note, God administers his saving life to us and through us. The word administers is where the word ministry is derived from. Have a think about it. As God administers his life through us, it is effectively being administered to another person. Could that be a definition of ministry? If so then we participate by becoming more and more like Jesus by living the transformation beatitudes, *open, empty, and detached.*

the family likeness, peace-making

Now we know that being called the children of God is because we are becoming recognisably more like him, we can talk about the peace-makers. If it hasn't dawned on you yet, becoming a peacemaker is an effect of becoming more like Jesus, arising from us living the first three beatitudes, so we can't just try to make peace, it won't work. Yeah, I think you guessed that.

Now we're ready to talk about peace-making. Tennis players have sports psychologists to train them, or if you like, disciple them, to come to a place of peace between each point. They cannot afford for their next point to be affected by the previous one. It's even more important when it's the last point, called the match point. They have to be able to approach this point from a place of peace just like every other point. Players have been known to be winning, and reach the last point, but are unable to win that point because the tension of the moment shortens their muscles as they tense up and they can't play their best shots.

It's the same with us in ordinary everyday life. As we engage with each event we are naturally affected by the previous event. We come to it, not from a place of peace, but influenced by what happened just before it. Sometimes influenced by what has happened repeatedly over time. Whilst this is natural and inevitable, it is a very poor way to live. The things that influence us from a previous event could be anger, prejudice, hurt, over-excitement, ambition, fear, threat, or just about anything. I hope you can see that this will corrupt the way we engage with the next moment, like with the tennis player on match point.

How often I have reacted and said something or sent a text message that I later regret. The brokenness or trauma from one event, possibly much earlier in time, can affect us into the future sometimes for hours, days, or even years. Equally, when something exciting happens or we experience some kind of gain or great pleasure, the following events can be affected by that. We can become giddy and perhaps lose sensitivity. The body chemistry is rightly pleasurable and uplifting. The drugs released by the brain into the body can however become addictive leading to compulsive habits to recreate the pleasure which is always diminished and pushing for more. Apparently, cycling enthusiasts can suffer from this through the adrenalin released by increasing amounts of challenge addictively sought. This has destructive effects on the psyche and their general health as some cycling enthusiasts have become aware.

my car again

Can I refer you back to my previous example of when that guy ran into my nearly new car? My initial engagement was clouded by the fear of suffering loss. This is something I often experience although I can't trace it back to a specific previous event. I compulsively needed to secure the outcome I felt was fair and just. However, over time I realised that the only way I could achieve that outcome was by seeking to prosecute the other driver and seriously affect his livelihood. My walk of openness to embrace my powerlessness to make the right outcome happen revealed the self-interest that was driving me. I found it strangely easy to self-empty my self-interest of entitlement, in the light of his potential loss. I found peace in letting him off, as the best course of action. Although he never knew it. I must admit that had my car damage been more substantial my peace may have been founded in justice and prosecution and that may have been the right action in that case.

the ups and the downs

One event being affected by previous events works both for the ups in life and for the downs. So, it's a known fact that rugby and football teams are most vulnerable to being scored against, immediately after scoring themselves. The high they experience from scoring affects the way they play immediately afterward. Coaches are well aware of this and give training for it, lest their team be vulnerable in this way.

We can't however train to recover from all the possible ups and downs in life so that we can be at peace before engaging with the next thing. The list would be endless. The problem here is that we don't naturally come to a place of peace between the events of everyday life like Jesus would, and like we will, as we become more like him. However, as we learn to live the first three beatitudes *of openness, emptiness, and detachment* we will become more like Jesus and will naturally/supernaturally find the place of peace between the events of everyday life.

We become the peacemakers because we have the peace of God in us that passes all understanding. Experiencing each moment of life from a place of peace, uncorrupted by previous events, is a wonder. It enables us to experience what Jesus promised, life in all its fullness in all circumstances; To engage in a life-giving way with the troubles of life and to fully experience the great pleasures of life we must become more like Jesus by living *openness, emptiness, and detachment.*

I've read about many ways to find the place of peace or the still point, and they were all good. Here we have Jesus giving us instruction on how we can automatically live our way to the place of peace by living as he would in *openness, emptiness and detachment.* When I meet someone who lives like this, I want to spend more time with them. I had a dear old friend who I spent time with regularly over the five or six years up to the time he passed away. Those times filled me with peace. He was a true peacemaker and lead me in the same direction.

So what I'm saying here is that we can become a peacemaker like Jesus; like my dear old friend, and engage in a peace that others can experience by following us in becoming more like Jesus. My old friend encouraged me endlessly to write things down for others to read, so here it is. He would have loved this book. Bless him.

11. CONTROL, THE ILLUSION AND THE LIE.

*the illusion is that you can have control
and the lie is that you need it.*

I think you've got the idea by now that the beatitudes that follow the first three, are the effects of living the first three, which fulfil Jesus' call on our lives to become more like Him. I'm going to share with you now, the conclusion I came to, that prompted the writing of this book. This chapter will offer a mirror to your experience of living everyday life. I'm guessing you will need to be open to seeing the authentic you, the real you. I'm hoping the journey we have been on in the previous chapters has walked you here.

Being open to your own powerlessness is being open to a power beyond yourself. God's power. It may well still be hard to realise your own powerlessness but unless it's faced, you may not be able to move on into a transformed experience of living. You will continue to live under the life-draining power of having to make life happen.

This, being open to my authentic self, for me, has been a repeated experience that gets easier and continues to bring a new kind of life into my everyday life. I now look forward to more and more revelations of the real me, the powerless me, that opens up more and more experiences of transformation.

control, the life-draining need for it, and breaking free.

We may believe that the only alternative to being in control is to lose control or to be out of control. But as we open the door to needing control, so the fear of losing control walks in and takes us prisoner. It's a self-imposed exile like all those exiles in the Old Testament. Exiles, or experiencing a wilderness, are hard times when reality bites, but they can also be times of renewal having reached the end of our rope. God rescues every time. Jesus is bringing God's rescue with the first three beatitudes of *openness, emptiness, and detachment* which when lived, will walk you out of this exile or wilderness experience of needing to have control and not getting it.

I sat listening to someone one day for quite a while and then said, "it sounds like you're lost in your own life". Most of the time we don't realise we're living lost in our own lives like this. We sort of get used to living a half-life of unmet expectations thinking this is all there is. The beatitudes are Jesus' main message to ordinary everyday people like us, and those on the side of that mountain that day, who are living a life that isn't life in all its fullness in all circumstances. The call is to walk in the way Jesus walks, in *openness, emptiness, and detachment* and as a result live life in all its fullness in all circumstances. I can't convince you; you just have to try it.

it's self-validating

The walk validates itself in your own experience. I've heard this time and time again from people who hear this message and try it. Some people say they understand it, agree with it but don't actually try it. It just becomes another one of those great Christian ideas they heard but never lived. The seed falls on rocky ground. Opening the door to needing control is understandable and is often triggered by really good intentions like to protect me and mine. This is especially true when you or yours are under threat.

Opening the door to needing control also occurs through the

compulsive desire to win or to be successful, neither of which you will find in the New Testament Kingdom of God. To win means someone loses, to be successful means someone is unsuccessful. I'm not saying you shouldn't play sport to win or to work hard to achieve your goals, I'm saying that ultimately you do not have control over that. In fact, the most pleasure is gained by playing to win or working hard towards your goals while being open to, and choosing, your own powerlessness to make it happen. And, if you do then do well in sport, or in your work goals, then celebrate.

Being open to, or choosing, your own powerlessness is also being open to a power beyond your own, which I believe is God's presence and power. Sound familiar. Sounds like freedom to me. Sounds like the poor in spirit in the first Beatitude. Sounds like Jesus. I'll talk more about this in the next chapter.

Whether the intentions of needing to have control over our lives are good or not so good, the illusion of control is however eventually broken by disillusionment; when we reach the end of our rope. It's painful, it hurts, it breaks us. We need this false version of ourselves that needs control, to be overtaken in a more life-giving way than total defeat. Jesus steps in with the beatitudes.

Every time we inadvertently pin our hopes on creating control over our circumstances, we are then living under the illusion that having control ourselves, is possible and necessary.

control, the illusion and the lie.

Breaking the need to have control is addressed by Jesus in the first beatitude, where we are invited to embrace our own powerlessness to make life happen, while still doing everything we can, but no more. It's not a call to do nothing, but we don't actually know what to do at all if we're closed to our own powerlessness and therefore closed to a power beyond our own. God's power. It seems important to me that Jesus starts here as he calls us to become more like him, to live freely and lightly. Being open to our own powerlessness to make life happen then, is the gateway. The journey of transformation begins here and it's here we will need to return every time we find ourselves tricked yet again into believing we can establish control over the circumstances of our lives.

a misunderstanding about control

It can simply be a misunderstanding about control. There is a need for control. There is control in the natural order. The illusion is that we can have control and the lie is that we need it. This illusion and lie of control is so potent that it tempts us with the power of being able to create control. Depending on whether you fight or flee, this lie will either fill you with the compulsive, obsessive dream of being able to create control or the fear that you absolutely need it but can't create it. Either way, we have given power over our lives to the illusion and lie of control.

breaking free, according to St Paul.

You can't actually break yourself free from the power of needing control, but God can and does, as we walk the way Jesus walked in the beatitudes. Remember Jesus is the way. I'm going to show you now, how St Paul explains to us what Jesus is saying in the first three beatitudes. Remember, *openness, emptiness, and detachment.*

Philippians 2:5-7. The New Jerusalem Bible says it well.

> *Make your own the mind of Christ Jesus: Who being in the form of God, did not count equality with God something to be grasped. But he emptied himself, taking on the form of a slave, becoming as human beings are; and being in every way like a human being.*

So here we have it from St Paul. "Make your own the mind of Christ Jesus". Other versions have it as … "you must have the mind of

Christ". It's possible. This is the call to become more like him, to think his thoughts and so speak his words and do what he would do in the circumstances of everyday life. Remember this is not about mission or ministry but about a new way of living everyday life. And the following is the way Paul says we do it.

> *v6 Being in the very form of God did not count equality with God something to be grasped.*

Jesus was in the form of God. He had the power to make life happen, but his way had to become the way we could take. Jesus chose to surrender his equality with God; his power to make life happen, and embraced powerlessness, to be like us so that we could walk the way he walked; a walk in a power beyond our own.

In the forty days in the wilderness, Matthew 4:1-11, the devil tempted Jesus to take back up his own power to make life happen by turning stones into bread, and he chose not to. Jesus resisted. The devil understood the incredibly life-destroying effect of the need for us to have control over our circumstances. Can you see how central it is to God that we also surrender the need to make life happen? And for us, we're only giving up an illusion; an illusion that will wreck our experience of living. Jesus chose to become the poor in spirit, dependant on a power beyond his own so that we could become like him and have the Kingdom of Heaven (power beyond our own) as he says in the first beatitude.

So, Paul here has totally validated the first beatitude about choosing powerlessness. He then goes further into the second beatitude.

> *v7 But, he (Jesus) emptied himself taking the form of a slave.*

Remember, the word used in the second beatitude as mourn is the word Paul uses here, kenos, empty. Jesus empties himself of every entitlement to power and control. (*Taking on the form of a slave*). A slave had no entitlement in their society. Here Jesus establishes the way for us to self-empty our self-interests and entitlements, so that we may become more like him. Remember, we don't self empty these things to become self-righteous, we self-empty them because if we keep them they will poison our experience of living because we will have given them power over us.

Finally, Paul talks about Jesus becoming the meek, detached from his own version of the outcomes and embracing God's outcomes.

> *v8 he (Jesus) was humbler yet, even unto death, death on a cross.*

This is the way Jesus walked; in openness to a power beyond his own by choosing to embrace powerlessness; in emptiness from all that could tempt him to try to make life happen on his own; and in detachment from the outcomes so that he could walk courageously into the outcomes God was creating.

It's been pointed out to me that it's really important to note that although Jesus chose powerlessness, he could in fact at any time, have taken back up his power to make things happen but he didn't. It's really important that we, whilst doing everything we can, choose powerlessness and do not revert to the illusion that we can take back up the power to make life happen; we are not divine in the same way Jesus is.

So, again I say it. Jesus is calling us in the first three beatitudes to walk through the circumstances of our daily lives the way he did and as a result, inherit life in all its fullness.

12. THEN CAME THE WIND

This chapter illustrates the illusion of control. When we were watching the tennis, the commentators were saying that this player was unbeatable. They went on and on about how perfect the player was. There wasn't anything that hadn't been mastered, everything was perfectly under control. I get fed up watching this player as the outcome is always an easy win. There had been a big build-up about how this match had to be won like all of the others. The player had been talking about it for days saying how important it was to journalists who lapped it up.

However, it was a windy day. The player in question was riled. Although the wind affected everybody the same and this player was tipped to win easily, the illusion of control was being challenged.

where needing to have control is relied upon,
the fear of losing control creeps in

And it did. I could see it all unfolding before my eyes. I wondered if anyone else saw it. The player shook a fist at the sky on international tv, defying the wind to challenge the control that had supposedly been established over years. So blinding to reality, is the need to have control over our circumstances ourselves.

The next shot was played and a gust of wind blew the ball just outside the reach of the racket and the point was lost. We all saw it. It was photographed and shown on news screens. It appeared on you-tube. The ball was clearly headed for the racket which was perfectly placed as usual and a gust of wind in that very moment blew the ball just outside of its reach.

*the illusion of having control and the lie of
needing it was unveiled in that moment.*

In my mind, the whole match was lost at that point. The illusion of control had been broken and the fear of losing control blinded the player with what looked like rage. Driven by rage, the player then lost the match and the tournament.

There was no reason for the match, to be lost. The player was still the favourite to win. But the match was lost and the dream of invincible winning, that the illusion of control had created, was also lost. I guess it was made all the worse by the commentators and news interviews beforehand, declaring that the level of control achieved by this player was unbreakable. In that moment I felt very sorry for the player.

I don't believe the wind defeated the player because everyone had to play in the wind and this player was better equipped to cope than any of them, apart from being sold out to the illusion of having control. I think the player was defeated by the illusion of having control and needing it, to win. The loss of control to the wind, appeared to steal the mind. It also seemed to steal the benefit of experience and skill.

Considering the circumstances of our everyday lives, where control seems the only way to get through, when control is inevitably lost, it seems there is no way through. We can become so blinded by the threat of loss of control, that what we may have been able to do, we now cannot do. Like the tennis player.

so how are we doing when the wind blows.

When the wind blows on our circumstances, how do we react? Some of us may try to stand up to the wind of circumstance in the hope of defeating it. Some of us may just give up in defeat, knowing we just can't stand against difficult times. Still others of us just stand in the wind of circumstance and let it batter us having no other alternative. I've done all of these and sometimes still do, sadly.

What happens when the wind blows on our needs; on the security of our family or on our dreams? Are we still holding out for the next thing we can do to sort it all? Are we still holding on to our entitlement for something and rehearsing how we might gain control to get the outcomes we feel we need?

I say these things because I've done them and sometimes still find myself there. It literally drains life from you and disables you from playing your part. In fact, the very actions we take to get us to where we feel we need to be can actually take us further away from that place. I have on my laptop screen saver, something Theresa of Avilla said.

"It's not the circumstances of everyday life that defeat or break us but the way we react to them".

reaction or response

Reaction is always the problem. When I react, it betrays the fact that I'm subconsciously relying on establishing my own control over my circumstances. It's as though somehow everything is down to me to get sorted. Reactions are unconsidered, immediate, sometimes necessary but mostly regretted. I can spot them now almost immediately and recover my steps.

So, when the wind blows on my circumstances, as I live the 'Jesus way' of the first three beatitudes, reaction is automatically replaced by response. The ability to respond as Jesus would if he were I. The transformative effect of being open to my powerlessness to make life happen enables me to see, and self-empty, the entitlements or needs that are driving me, and I can then become detached from the outcomes I desperately felt I needed, that would have been controlling me. I'm then free to respond in a life giving way when the wind blows on my circumstances. Without my beatitudes walk, I'm still captive to my destructive reactions like the tennis player.

Once we've begun walking the beatitudes into our lives, the response, instead of reaction, to our circumstances can be immediate, because we are becoming the kind of person that doesn't react. Someone recently said to me .... the difficult circumstances of life are the same and they keep coming but I find that I am different".

I once was blind but now I see

I find that as this transformation journey begins, my engagement with the circumstances of everyday life is bolder, more courageous, more intimate, more focussed, and wiser. I am able to see the things that can be done, that I couldn't see before, and I'm able to find life in my circumstances whatever they are.

13. THE PRACTICE OF GIVING WAY

This final chapter reveals that Jesus was retelling his message of the beatitudes when he told the story of the prodigal son. Or at least that's what I'd like to propose to you and make clear by the end of this chapter.

The message in the prodigal son is the call to become more like the father in the story, and as a result, live freely and lightly just as Jesus says in Matthew 11:28-30 MSG.

This chapter is a teaching I gave more recently and three years after my journey into the beatitudes began. It is the place I have arrived at over those three years and a place I offered to the congregation at that time. It's a message that has come out of a real-life journey with a community of people so it's had the tests of how we can live the beatitudes in everyday life. A journey from complexity to simplicity. So can I offer you this final message as a summary and destination of our journey through this book? Though I say destination, it is and always will be, a step on the ongoing journey of transformation to become more like Jesus, and will lead to other steps that you and I will take as we continue this lifelong pilgrimage to become more like him.

Can I give you this message as I gave it and hopefully you will see echoes from the previous chapters, which to us, were the previous years of the journey? It's a long chapter so please make yourself comfortable.

giving way – the message I gave.

I'm going to introduce the practice of giving way.

Giving way, to make way, for a much better way. Making way for God. I'd like to propose to us that Jesus' calling on our lives is to become more and more like him. ...

.... The one who is able to embrace life in all circumstances, live life in all its fullness and bring the life of God to all things.

Please note those three things; *able to embrace life in all circumstances, live life in all its fullness, and bring the life of God to all things.* These are all things Jesus is saying we will be able to do.

The hymn writer has it.

Breathe on me, breath of God:
fill me with life anew,
that I may love as you have loved
and do as you would do.

Breathe on me, breath of God,
until my heart is pure,
until my will is one with yours
to do and to endure.

Breathe on me, breath of God;
so shall I never die,
but live with you the perfect life
of your eternity.

The theology is beautiful. The hymn writer doesn't say we can engage with life as Jesus would, and live this life anew, by trying harder to think and act as Jesus would. He says we do it by the breath of God which transforms us to become more like Jesus.

Can you see the transformation to become like him, here?

> ... *"that I may love as you have loved and do as you would do"*,
> *"until my will is one with yours".*

Also, can you also see living life in all its fullness...

> *"but live with you the perfect life".*

The hymn writer has definitely caught our meaning.

the great good news.

Jesus' great good news then, the gospel if you like, is that we are called to become more and more like him and as a result be able to *embrace life in all circumstances, live life in all its fullness, and bring the life of God to all things.*

Those three things again from before. Note they include: transformation (*able to embrace life in all circumstances*); celebration of life (*live life in all its fullness*); And if you like, purpose, mission or ministry, or whatever you may call it. (*bring the life of God to all things*).

After 27 years of pastoral ministry, I tend to steer clear of well-used Christian words like witness, mission, and ministry as they can bring so much baggage with them which can cloud what's really happening for us now and cause some to turn away because of previous experiences. So, I prefer to say that a life being transformed to become more like Jesus is an enjoyable, attractive kind of life (witness), and a life that will overflow and bring life into the world (purpose, mission, or ministry).

the story of the prodigal son is an illustration of the beatitudes to show us what it looks like in real life.

Jesus here shows us how to take this journey of becoming more like him, in the beatitudes, from his sermon on the mount. He also shows us even more simply how to become more like him, in the story of the prodigal son.

The father in the story is the one who is able to *embrace life in all circumstances, live life in all its fullness, and bring the life of God to all things.* (those three things again)

a story of transformation told by Jesus.

Of course, Jesus is describing himself here as the father, the one we are to become like, and he uses the actions of the father in the story to show how we become like him. So yes, I'm saying that the story of the prodigal is a story showing what a journey of transformation looks like for us.

We begin as the younger son, possibly become the older son, and finally are called to be transformed to become like the father. Like Jesus.

People say to me, that isn't the father in the story supposed to be God. Well, you could say that and then remember that Jesus is the perfect representation of God on earth. Hebrews 1:3. And, Jesus is our way to the Father. So can we now say that in the story, Jesus is describing his 'way' when he describes the 'way' of the father?

Jesus is repeatedly describing himself so that we know where we're headed in becoming more like him.

I realise that throughout this book I've invited us to see that Jesus is describing himself repeatedly. As I showed us in the bible study from Paul, Jesus is the poor in spirit, he is those who mourn/self-empty and he is the meek of the first three beatitudes. He is the open, empty, and detached one.

the story of the prodigal son, or is it story of becoming like the life-giving father.

I've included the first part of the story here to show you how I arrived at this message. Luke 15 NIV. 11

Jesus continued: "There was a man who had two sons. 12 The younger one said to his father, 'Father, give me my share of the estate.' So he divided his property between them. 13 "Not long after that, the younger son got together all he had, set off for a distant country and there squandered his wealth in wild living. 14 After he had spent everything, there was a severe famine in that whole country, and he began to be in need. 15 So he went and hired himself out to a citizen of that country, who sent him to his fields to feed pigs. 16 He longed to fill his stomach with the pods that the pigs were eating, but no one gave him anything. 17 "When he came to his senses, he said, 'How many of my father's hired servants have food to spare, and here I am starving to death! 18 I will set out and go back to my father and say to him: Father, I have sinned against heaven and against you. 19 I am no longer worthy to be called your son; make me like one of your hired servants.' 20 So he got up and went to his father. "But while he was still a long way off, his father saw him and was filled with compassion for him; he ran to his son, threw his arms around him and kissed him. 21 "The son said to him, 'Father, I have sinned against heaven and against you. I am no longer worthy to be called your son.' 22 "But the father said to his servants, 'Quick! Bring the best robe and put it on him. Put a ring on his finger and sandals on his feet. 23 Bring the fattened calf and kill it. Let's have a feast and celebrate. 24 For this son of mine was dead and is alive again; he was lost and is found.' So they began to celebrate.

the make life happen, younger son.

The younger son, who goes away, believes he can make life happen without his father. He believes that if he doesn't make life happen for himself then it won't happen. Does this sound familiar. Remember the 'make it happen barrier' of the first beatitude.

Also, remember on this journey from complexity to simplicity the younger son is us.

This illusion and lie that he can have, and needs, full control over his life, is driving him to take on the full burden of making life happen. As I say he is us.

Jesus is in effect saying, here is the start point on the journey of transformation.

Naturally, we believe it's down to us to make life happen for us and for ours. We may either grab and push to make life happen, work endlessly and often blindly to make life happen, or be fearful we can't make life happen. These are all the same human condition. For the son, it's a life without his father. It's the same for us, remember we begin as the younger son.

So how does the father in the story engage with this son? Remember this is a journey Jesus is taking us on, to become less like the son and more like the father in the story.

The son has just demanded his inheritance from his father, while his father is still alive. In their culture, this was a shameful thing to do. Does the father agree with what is happening, no; does he want it, no; does he condone it, no; does he accept it, no; does he battle with what is happening, no; does he give in to it as helpless, no; does he just give up as hopeless, no. You may want to reflect on each of these as they will be occurring in the way we engage with the circumstances of everyday life. There is an alternative for the meek, here it is.

He doesn't battle, give in or give up, he gives way. I said at the beginning I would introduce us to the power of giving way, and in giving way, the father in the story makes way for a better way, the power of God in his circumstances. This is how the father becomes the *one who can embrace life in all circumstances, live life in all its fullness, and bring the life of God into all things.*

the father doesn't battle, give in or give up, he gives way.

Firstly, the father gives way to the younger son's request for half of the estate. This giving way is a clear embrace of the circumstances even though they are extremely difficult. It would have been shameful for a son to request his inheritance before the death of his father. It may even have been interpreted as the son wishing his father dead. Jesus is pitching the breadth of this embrace, as very wide indeed.

The father doesn't want this circumstance, he doesn't condone it, he doesn't accept it, and he doesn't battle with what is happening. He doesn't give in to it as helpless and he doesn't just give up as hopeless? He doesn't battle, give in or give up he gives way.

the father becomes the poor in spirit of the first beatitude.

The father surrenders his own power over the circumstances (he becomes the poor in spirit) and in effect relinquishes any control he may have tried to exercise over what's happening. So, the father is able to embrace life in all circumstances by giving way, to make way for God's presence and power. Do you recognise him? He is Paul's Jesus from Philippians 2:5-7.

Secondly, the father lives life in all its fullness in all circumstances. Having given way to make way for God's way, the father in turn lives life in all its fullness when he later embraces the younger son again. Here it is from the text.

> "But while he was still a long way off, his father saw him and was filled with compassion for him; he ran to his son, threw his arms around him and kissed him. 21 "The son said to him, 'Father, I have sinned against heaven and against you. I am no longer worthy to be called your son.' 22 "But the father said to his servants, 'Quick! Bring the best robe and put it on him. Put a ring on his finger and sandals on his feet. 23 Bring the fattened calf and kill it. Let's have a feast and celebrate. 24 For this son

of mine was dead and is alive again; he was lost and is found.'
So they began to celebrate"

what can't you see here?

Can you see any evidence in the father whatsoever of recrimination or judgment? No. Can you see any regret or disappointment? No. Do you get the idea that the father is going to bring this up at a later date? No. These things are conspicuously absent in the text for a reason. We would expect to see them and they're not there.

Considering the loss of money, the shame, and the sheer worry he has been through, is the father living hurt with the injury of what the son has done to him? No. This is clearly, living freely and lightly and living life in all its fullness in all circumstances. The father is clearly Jesus who we are being journeyed to become like.

what can you see?

Thirdly, can you see how the father sowed the life of God into his younger son, by giving way to the circumstance? In the story, as Jesus told it, the father spoke no words as his son left. His actions spoke for him. When the father gave way to the son, his actions sowed into the son the power of giving way to make way for God's way. Remember the father is Jesus and so, full of grace. And also remember Jesus is calling us to become more like him.

I'm pretty sure in that moment the son was probably conscious of just one thing; getting away with the money and making life happen for himself, separate from his father. However, when the son came to the end of his rope, the seed had taken root and the son was able to give way to his own circumstances. The son could have pressed on stubbornly, or given up defeated never to return to his father. But instead, the son gave way to his circumstances and as a result of that, found his way back home to his father. The son realised he was powerless to make his life happen, and he also realised his actions were a sin against his father and against heaven.

Giving way, made way, for this realisation, and his father had shown him what it looks like to give way to difficult circumstances. So can you now see how the father sowed the life of God into his younger son, by giving way, and how that seed of life took root and saved the son from himself?

If you are a parent or someone who has sown the life of God into another, you will be aware that in the moment it can look like nothing has taken root. A bit like in the son who went off to make life happen for himself. In my mind, it's a necessary journey that we probably all take at some point in our lives. What I can say, is that those seeds of life will have been sown, and in time they will come up as a new kind of life as and when the recipient gives soil to them.

I have just demonstrated how the actions of the father in the story reveal what he was like.

He was able *to embrace life in all circumstances, live life in all its fullness, and bring the life of God into all things.* Embrace, live, and bring life to another. What a calling. What a wonderful kind of life. This is the one Jesus is calling us to become like and he has shown us clearly how.

it begins by practicing giving way, here is how.

When we give way as the circumstances of life come upon us, we don't have to like the circumstance, or condone it, or accept it, or battle against what is happening. We don't have to give in to it as helpless or just give up as hopeless. We don't have to battle, give in or give up, we can, like the father in the story, give way. Giving way is getting real. It's how we manage to live in the truth of the moments that come to us. It's authentic living.

As we give way we realise, or become open to, our powerlessness to make life happen. (we become the poor in spirit, like Jesus) and in effect relinquish any control we wanted over what's happening. We will automatically self-empty any vested interests we have that are poisoning us (mourn/kenos/empty) and detach ourselves from the outcomes we're holding out for, that will be controlling us. (the meek). This is how Jesus is saying we can become more like him. Giving way, makes way, for a better way, that comes by the presence and power of God in our lives. Can you now see the relationship between the beatitudes and the story of the prodigal son?

> *the older son thought he could earn the*
> *right to live the life of his father.*

When I gave this message, a guy in the coffee break at church said to me "the father also 'gave way' to the older son who stayed at home, but the story ends with us not knowing if the older son responded." The older son had stayed at home when the younger son left, but he still took into his own hands the power to make his life happen. This time by earning it. The older son thought he could earn the right to live the life of his father, when, in reality, only transformation to become like his father would have got him there. When the party begins for the return of his younger brother, the older son refuses to enter on the basis of the unmet entitlement he's been slaving for, and his father gives way by pleading with him to come in. Here it is in the text.
Luke 15:28 NIV

> *"The older brother became angry and refused to go in. So his father went out and pleaded with him. 29 But he answered his father, 'Look! All these years I've been slaving for you and never disobeyed your orders. Yet you never gave me even a young goat so I could celebrate with my friends. 30 But when this son of yours who has squandered your property with prostitutes comes home, you kill the fattened calf for him!"*

The older son thought that by doing things for his father he could earn, and be entitled to, the privileged life of his father. In our terms, he thought he could live the life of Jesus by doing things for him as opposed to becoming more like him.

According to Jesus, it's in becoming more like him, that we will be able to live his kind of life which automatically sows the life of God into those around us, into our families, our communities, society, and the world. The world is watching and waiting for us to become like him, to love like he does because we are becoming more like him. The older son missed the practice of giving way that was being lived out by his father. Instead, he took the path of making his own way by working for his father for a reward as opposed to becoming more like him, by giving way and joining the party.

it's all about inheritance

Note, the younger and older son were attempting to inherit the privileged life of their father by their own means, when all along all they needed to do was to become more like him. They would have inherited as his sons, those who bear the father's likeness, but their actions to make inheritance happen by their own means defeated the very thing they had set out to make happen. Have a think about that for our own lives. How often do our efforts to make something happen, defeat the very thing we're looking for? As we take the beatitudes pathway, we will automatically become like him and inherit a new kind of life that lives well in all circumstances. Which is just what we're looking for. It's no mistake that in the third beatitude, the text says, the meek inherit the earth. Note inherit.

I just need to say a few things to help with questions that may arise.

I'm aware that the story Jesus told about the prodigal son is heavily laden with meaning and teaching I have not dealt with. I'm picking up the overall message, of Jesus calling us to become like the father, like himself, and showing us how by the simple practice of giving way.

I'm also aware that the idea of giving way will not sit easily with us. It sounds like giving in or giving up which I hope I have demonstrated that it is not. I'll illustrate this in the following section with how it is working for me.

will you try the Jesus way, to become more like him by practicing giving way?

One way for me, in learning to give way, has been to give myself permission to be infirm where I am infirm. To give way to my infirmity. Not to deny it or battle onward to defeat it. Not giving up or giving in to it, but giving way. Its facing reality instead of running away from it. Bear in mind that the only place we can experience God is in reality, so why hide from it, deny it, or run away from it.

I know it can be painful, but you will meet God there if you give way to reality. Giving way to make way for God to move. Just like the father in Jesus' story. Try battling onward against infirmity by walking on a broken leg or standing against anxiety. It will be excruciating and will make things worse. Freedom and healing begin as we learn to give way to our infirmities and discover God's way through them. Could that be a definition of healing?

giving way and my behaviour

Giving way to my infirmities has revealed to me why I sometimes behave like I do, and has resulted in me not expecting too much of myself in certain circumstances. I don't weaponize the infirmity by allowing myself to do whatever I like. I give way to it and become open to God's way to engage with it. You may need to give way to an infirmity like anger or rage by giving yourself permission to be angry. The immediate question is, does this mean I can just be angry when it suits me. No, that would weaponize the anger as an excuse for abusive behaviour, by giving anger power over you. It means that the reality for you in that moment is anger, and giving yourself permission to be how you are is an act of embracing your circumstances. You will meet God's healing presence there.

because we can only experience God
is in the present moment.

The reason why this is important is because although God exists in the past, the future, and the present, you can only experience God in the present moment. This is because you are not in the past, or the future, you are only in the present moment. If we avoid, deny, or run away from the present moment, however difficult it is, we run away from the only place we can experience God. There was a time when the only prayer we knew was "God get me out of here". However, if we can embrace our current circumstance as reality for us, then we will meet God there and the deliverance and healing can begin.

giving way raises our consciousness.

This has relieved me from having to just try harder to make life happen when clearly, I can't. I've become more conscious of why I behave the way I do, and I'm engaging with the circumstances of life in a more life-giving way than I was before. Perhaps more like Jesus would if he were I. Living as Jesus says in Matthew, more freely and lightly.

Giving way is not a weak thing to do, it takes faith. It means facing up to things the way they really are but not taking on the burden to make life happen, just like the father in the story. Like Jesus. It takes faith to give way, trusting that in doing so we will make way for God's way to be revealed to us. This is what I mean by raised consciousness. As we give way to things as they are, we are released from the need to stand against them, or fix them, or run from them. The relief from all this psychological traffic clears our psyche, or mind, or spirit whatever you call it. The clearing makes us conscious of new possibilities that I believe come from God. I also have experienced that this increased consciousness makes me aware of deeper attachments I may have to make things happen or just deeper infirmities, all of which I can now give way to. Guess what, this further giving way raises consciousness again to even deeper growth and healing.

giving way is meek, not weak.

Jesus calls those who learn to give way, the meek, who by the way, according to Jesus, inherit the earth. Matthew 5:5

Blessed are the meek for they shall inherit the earth.

They inherit what they were previously either fighting for or have given up on. Note in the beatitudes, Jesus uses the term "shall inherit the earth" about the meek, which as I mentioned earlier is the background of the story of the prodigal son.

The meek by the way, who inherit the earth, are those who learn to give way, to make way, for God's way. Jesus is yet again describing himself as the meek. Remember I illustrated in the bible study from Philippians, that Jesus gave way, to make way, for God's way. Not my way but yours.

fulfilling the calling on our lives.

In learning to give way in my days like the father did, I'm fulfilling the calling on my life to become more like Jesus, and as a result, I'm engaging with everyday life more like he would if he were I. I'm learning to give way in other ways too. I'm learning to give way to the people in my life, to make way for God to move in my relationship with them and for God to move in their lives. To give way sometimes to the circumstances I find myself in rather than fighting for a way through or giving up. I know that every time I give way, I find a new way to engage, a way previously unknown to me, a way that enables me to embrace life in all circumstances, live life in all its fullness, and bring the life of God to things. Ring any bells?

14. OVER TO YOU NOW

So, I close where I began. In the first three transformational beatitudes, Jesus is revealing to us how we can become more like him, and be able to embrace life in all circumstances, live life in all its fullness, and sow the life of God into the world around us just as he does.

Becoming more like Jesus then is his primary calling on our lives and everything else flows from this. Seek first the Kingdom of God and all else will follow. MATTHEW 6:33.

Jesus gives us the simple way in the first three transformational beatitudes, which are the way he takes, and the way we will take if we want to respond to his call to become more like him and live freely and lightly in this world.

Here they are, and finally.

the blessed place of openness, the first beatitude

Firstly, as the circumstances of life come upon us, good or ill, we are to become open to a power greater than our own, by realising our own powerlessness to make life happen while still doing everything we can but no more. In being open to our powerlessness we become conscious of new possibilities which I call becoming open to God's presence and power in our circumstances.

The beauty of this place is that we experience the presence of God and God experiences our presence. In this blessed place of openness, our consciousness increases, and our minds become clear from all the cloudiness and confusion, because we are no longer winding ourselves up by seeking control over our circumstances. This is a place of rest and makes us ready for the second beatitude. Remember as I showed you in Paul's letter to the Philippians, Jesus walked this way.

the blessed place of emptiness, the second beatitude.

Secondly, being in a place of rest and open to God's presence enables us to see the things we have allowed into our hearts and minds to try to make life happen for us and ours. These things like entitlement, hurt, or just the sheer compelling need to get sorted, poison our experience of daily life. However, once the poisoning effect of these things is revealed we will naturally want to empty ourselves of them.

The text uses the words, blessed are those who mourn, and we now know that mourn is kenos, empty. This is the blessed place of emptiness where we are held by God instead of the things in our hearts. Remember the things we hold onto will hold us.

detachment, the third beatitude.

Thirdly, we are now ready for the third beatitude; to be detached from the things we were holding onto and the outcomes they falsely promise. Jesus emptied himself. Being open to a power greater than our own, that I call God's presence and power, and empty of all that holds us, we will be able to detach ourselves from the outcomes we felt we needed to make life happen for us and ours. Once detached from the outcomes we thought we needed, we are able to see and engage with new possibilities that will surely be revealed to us. The describes those who are at peace with relinquishing their hold over the outcomes in life as, the meek. Matthew 5:5

Jesus again is describing himself as the meek and who we are to become more like. Not my way but yours.

Control, the illusion and the lie.

The illusion is that we can have control over our lives and the lie is that we need it.

The whole thing is about us wrongly believing that we can have control over our lives, and need that control, believing that it's down to us to make life happen or things will go terribly out of control. Holding on to entitlement and our needs and desires to make life happen is about control. And attaching ourselves to the outcomes we feel we need is about control. The belief that we can have control is a tempting illusion, and the lie that we need control becomes an obsessive compulsion.

Practicing living the first three transformation beatitudes of openness, emptiness, and detachment, breaks us free from the illusion that we can have control ourselves over our lives and rescues us from the lie that we need it.

In the end, Jesus saves us from ourselves
by saying ....

"come and see"

ABOUT THE AUTHOR

Gary Smith

I'm a married man with two grown-up children and three grandchildren.

I spent 25 years working in industry and commerce, starting at the bottom and culminating in managing a business for a major company. Towards the end of this time, I began a season of planting and pastoring a church with my wife, from which we retired after 27 years of pastoral ministry.

For both of these seasons of my life, in the main, I have experienced an easy yoke and a light burden. This is mainly due to the fact that I don't consider myself to be particularly well qualified or well educated, so I have always had to rely on a wisdom and power greater than my own. I have realised many, many times over that I can't make life happen either in employment, pastoral ministry, or in family life. This resulted in a constant search for the ability to engage with life well, in all circumstances, through my life with God. A faith in God for me then had to be able to be lived, in all the experiences of everyday life, in every area of life. There was never any place for theory.

The way I tick is that I believe people live much better if they are helped and guided to make their own choices in the everyday circumstances of life. The textbooks might call it equipped, envisioned, empowered, and released. It's really about honouring all people, adults and children alike. Therefore, there has never been any place for me in trying to get others to do what I wanted them to do, in the household, employment, or the church. This has been the nature of my life with God as he constantly equips, envisions, empowers, and releases me, as and when I am able to realise my own powerlessness to make life happen.

At the time of writing in 2022, I am in my 70th year. After all this time, for me, the simple way of being able to live God's kind of life is to become more and more like him. However, I could never leave you without showing you how we can become more like him. Having read this book, you will not be surprised that I believe Jesus shows us how to become more like him in the first three beatitudes by living open, empty, and detached, just as he did.

Live well.

Printed in Great Britain
by Amazon

16152906R00078